Mountain Biking

NEW
HOLLAND

Mountain Biking

Susanna & Herman Mills

NEW
HOLLAND

First published in 2000 by
New Holland Publishers Ltd
London • Cape Town • Sydney • Auckland

24 Nutford Place
London W1H 6DQ
United Kingdom

80 McKenzie Street
Cape Town 8001
South Africa

14 Aquatic Drive
Frenchs Forest, NSW 2086
Australia

218 Lake Road
Northcote, Auckland
New Zealand

ISBN 1 85974 458 3 (hardcover)
ISBN 1 85974 401 X (softcover)

Publisher: Mariëlle Renssen
Commissioning editor: Claudia Dos Santos
Managing editor: Sean Fraser
Designer: Gillian Black
Illustrator: Danie Jansen van Vuuren
Production: Myrna Collins

Consultant (UK): John Kitchiner (*MBR* Magazine)

Reproduction by Hirt & Carter (Cape) Pty Ltd
Printed and bound in Singapore by Craft Print (Pte) Ltd

Although the authors and publishers have made every effort
to ensure that the information in this book was correct at
the time of going to press, they accept no responsibility for
any loss, injury or inconvenience sustained by any person
using the information contained herein.

Publisher's acknowledgements
The publisher would like to thank the
principal photographer, Jacques Marais,
and the individuals and institutions that
offered assistance: Gui Gouws, Indola
Apparel, Hopkins Cycle Inn, the Sports
Science Institute (Cape Town), Dirtopia
(Greyton), and the Montagu Tourism Board.

Authors' acknowledgements

'In his heart a man plans his course, but the Lord determines his steps.' *Proverbs 16:9*

We would like to dedicate this work to our parents Justinus and Embrencia Mills, and Kenneth and Betty Morrison, who taught us to believe in ourselves and equipped us for life by investing so much in us — spiritually, morally and educationally. Now that we are parents ourselves, we appreciate you even more! Thanks must also go to Ian Martin, sports scientist, training expert and roadie for his contribution, Chapter 5. We'll get you dirty yet...

Of course, we would also like to thank the editorial and design team at Struik New Holland who helped to transform our manuscript into a remarkable book. To them and all who contributed, our sincerest thanks.

Contents

Ride your Bike

no matter what your motivation, mountain biking comes neatly wrapped in a versatile package that fulfils many of your needs.

Where did it all start?

Mountain biking originated in California in the early 1970s, and Mount Tamalpais — or Mt Tam, as it is better known — is widely regarded as the birthplace of mountain biking. Thousands of enthusiasts have made their way to that magic mountain, 'paying homage' to the early pioneers who had the vision and determination to go against popular cycling opinion. They converted old cruisers and balloon-tyre bicycles into human-powered machines capable of surviving off-road conditions, and individuals such as Gary Fisher, Charlie Cunningham,

Keith Bontrager, Tom Ritchey, and others, are hailed as the founding fathers of the sport. Initially, they ferried their bikes up the mountain on trucks, and raced them down. To stop, they used old-style coaster brakes and, during descents, these old braking systems heated up so much that the grease melted, and the rear hub had to be re-packed with grease before the next downhill run. (The name 'repack' became synonymous with a particular downhill on Pine Mountain.) These 'retro' bikes were heavy, single-speed clunkers, adapted with parts cannibalized from small motorcycles and mopeds. Soon riders felt that, in order to enjoy the ride down, you had to earn the right by riding up first. This then resulted in a cottage industry, creating bikes with gears and shifters that could achieve this — thus laying the foundation for the corporations we know today.

As the sport grew in popularity, bicycle-component manufacturers began to take notice. Soon mountain bike-specific groupsets became available, further developing the new industry. Mountain bikes currently outsell road bikes at a ratio of about 5:1. But much has changed since the 1970s, and today you can buy a top-quality dual-suspension composite bike with disc brakes and light, but strong components made from exotic alloys, relatively cheaply compared to road bicycles. There are few rules and organizers are generally relaxed about those that have been instituted. The gap between casual and professional riders has now widened so much that a licensing system separates professionals from amateurs. In future, even further specialization by top riders will take performance to another level. This, in turn, will drive the refinement of components, which will consequently improve the mainstream equipment available.

EARLY OFF-ROAD PIONEERS, SUCH AS GARY FISHER, HAD THE VISION AND DETERMINATION TO GO AGAINST POPULAR CYCLING OPINION.

opposite ONCE YOU HAVE BEGUN TO RIDE YOUR BICYCLE OFF-ROAD REGULARLY, EVERY RIDE BECOMES AN ADVENTURE.

Getting Equipped

although mountain bikes evolved from the fat-tyre cruiser bikes popular in the 1960s, progress has been so rapid that advances in mountain-bike technology are seen, in some cases, to have overtaken Formula-One technology.

High-tech frame materials

A bicycle frame needs to withstand a wide variety of stresses from many sources. Braking, pedalling and shocks from the terrain are but a few forces that influence frames. The material, construction and design are thus vital in creating an efficient and reliable bike.

Aluminium alloys

Manufacturers produce a variety of aluminium alloys, and names such as Easton Aluminium, Alpha, Columbus, and Reynolds are synonymous with these tubesets. Of course, most bike companies have tubing made to their own specifications. Properly designed aluminium frames offer important advantages, such as light weight, high resistance to corrosion, and low cost. They are also easier to manufacture because the tubes can be drawn, mitered and dressed in almost any shape. The completed frame usually offers superior rigidity,

which is crucial in the construction of full-suspension bikes. This is especially true when wide-diameter, oversized tubing is used, such as those on Cannondale and many other bikes. Aluminium, in its raw form of aluminium oxide, is also one of the most abundant metals on earth.

Composites

Composite materials, such as carbon fibre and Kevlar composites, have proven themselves as a viable and highly successful frame and component material. The major advantage is the ability of the manufacturer to manipulate the raw materials in such a way as to produce specific characteristics where these are required. This process also produces a remarkably light frame and, since it is essentially built in a mould, the usual constraints enforced by pre-manufactured tubing do not exist. The frames can be produced in any shape and size the designer desires. The most important drawback of composite frames, however, is that they are impossible to repair, and are sensitive to degradation if exposed to chemicals, such as solvents and acids. Manufacturing processes may be very complicated, such as TREK's patented OCLV (Optimum Compaction Low Void) technology. However, although expensive, a carbon-fibre frame is both durable and light.

'Next generation' frames

The recent trend is to construct frames using a combination of materials. Cannondale, for example, uses an aluminium endoskeleton or backbone, with a carbon-fibre exoskeleton. Raleigh constructed

Why and when to upgrade

Why and when to upgrade depends on how frequently you use your bike, and what you enjoy using it for. If you are enthusiastic about mountain biking and riding off-road gives you a great deal of pleasure and fulfilment, you may want to have the best equipment you can buy to take your experience of it even further. You may also become interested in being competitive, and for this you will not only need a body that performs, but a high-performance bicycle too.

opposite DOWNHILL OR CROSS COUNTRY? ENDURANCE OR TECHNICAL SKILLS? BEFORE YOU BUY A BIKE AND ACCESSORIES — FIRST DECIDE WHAT YOU INTEND TO DO WITH THEM.

bikes from carbon-fibre tubes, which were glued onto titanium lugs. Carbon-fibre frames, with a honeycomb structure between layers of carbon fibre, offer a frame that is light and strong, yet still competitively priced.

Steel alloys

Steel was once the traditional material for the construction of bicycles. Companies such as Reynolds, Columbus, Tange, and True Temper still manufacture top-quality tubesets for bicycle frames. Carbon-steel tubing is usually used in most entry-level bikes, while chrome molybdenum, and chrome manganese are used in a butted format on selected high-end bikes. Despite

TODAY'S MOUNTAIN BIKE IS A RESULT OF DEVELOPMENTS IN TECHNOLOGY. ONE INNOVATION IS CANNONDALE'S UNCONVENTIONAL 'LEFTY' FORK. THE EFFICIENT, MODERN EQUIPMENT SIMPLY ADDS TO THE FUN.

it not being 'fashionable', steel still offers some unique properties. A steel bike feels alive; with its inherent shock absorption and exceptional strength-to-weight ratio, it is rivalled only by titanium alloys in certain areas. Furthermore, unlike more exotic materials, steel is easily repaired.

Titanium alloys

Titanium alloy is often the material of choice for top-quality lightweight frames. However, titanium is not only as good as the best steel alloys, but it is also abrasion and corrosion resistant, and produces a frame that truly looks high-tech. These framesets are quite expensive, but exceptionally durable.

The anatomy of a mountain bike

The modern mountain bike can be identified by its specialist frameset — designed to cope with the high-impact environment of off-road cycling.

The frame and handlebars

To allow for easier handling, the angles of the mountain-bike frame are quite relaxed. The frame also needs to be smaller than that of a road bike for the same rider. This is to allow for the ideal set-up for off-road riding, which is necessary for agility over a variety of surfaces.

Flat handlebars with bar-end extensions are now standard, although riser bars have recently gained popularity, mostly due to the comfortable upright riding position they provide, but also thanks to fashion.

Gears and brakes

In order to climb steep hills, mountain-bike gears have extraordinary ratios. Gear-shifting systems have undergone considerable development in recent years, and today the Grip Shift and RapidFire designs are the most prominent.

Disc brakes have developed at such a rate — and are so efficient — that they are already available on most high-end bikes, either as standard equipment or as an option. However, traditional rim brakes still offer good braking efficiency.

Cranks and derailleurs

Usually made from a lightweight aluminium alloy, cast or cold-forged into shape, cranks may also be made from a composite, with metal inserts at critical points.

The function of the derailleurs — the French word for 'redirect' or 'derail' — depends on the gear ratio initiated with your handlebar-mounted gear shifters.

Saddle

Although the saddle is one of the few points on the bike that has direct contact with your body, manufacturers often compromise with an inferior saddle, so consider buying the best saddle you can afford. The modern anatomically correct saddles for men and women provide improved comfort and less chance of injury.

Pedals

Pedals may or may not be equipped with special toe clips, plastic or metal cages that allow you to strap your feet into the pedal. Clipless pedals and shoes will increase your power transfer substantially.

Wheels

Special high-performance wheels have become popular, largely due to the wheels' high efficiency and light weight — but beware of sacrificing the strength of your equipment just to lose a few grams.

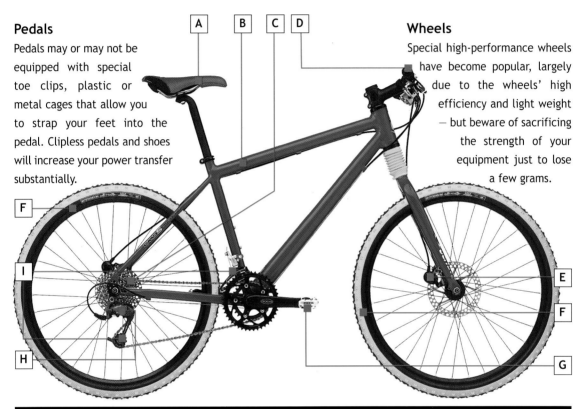

A SADDLE: SADDLE DESIGN HAS IMPROVED GREATLY, AND THE NEW GENERATION OF ERGONOMICALLY CORRECT SADDLES NOW PROVIDES ADDITIONAL COMFORT, ALLEVIATING INJURIES CAUSED BY SADDLE PRESSURE.

B FRAME: THE MODERN MOUNTAIN-BIKE FRAME COMPENSATES FOR ADDITIONAL HEIGHT FROM THE FORK BY INCORPORATING A SLOPING TOP-TUBE.

C GEARS: ALTHOUGH THE TRANSITION FROM 24- TO 27-SPEED HAS MET WITH MIXED REACTIONS, MANY 21-SPEED BIKES ARE AVAILABLE — EVEN IF THEY ARE NO LONGER STOCKED BY RETAILERS.

D HANDLEBARS: RISER BARS HAVE RECENTLY GAINED POPULARITY, MOSTLY DUE TO A MORE COMFORTABLE UPRIGHT RIDING POSITION.

E BRAKES: BRAKING WAS ONCE ACHIEVED BY USING CANTILEVER BRAKES, BUT NOW LINEAR PULL-TYPE 'BRAKES' ARE STANDARD ISSUE ON MOST BIKES, AND DISC BRAKES ARE AVAILABLE ON MOST MEDIUM- TO HIGH-END MODELS.

F WHEELS: MOUNTAIN BIKES MAY BE DEFINED BY THEIR 70CM/26IN WHEELS. MOST BIKES STILL USE ALLOY RIMS WITH 36, 32, OR 28 SPOKES INSTALLED IN A STANDARD THREE-CROSS CONFIG-URATION OR RADIAL CONFIGURATION IN FRONT.

G PEDALS: CLIPLESS PEDALS FOR MOUNTAIN BIKES HAVE BEEN PERFECTED OVER THE LAST SIX YEARS, AND ARE NOW THE CHOICE OF MOST SERIOUS RIDERS.

H CRANKS: SOME OF THE LATEST DESIGNS USE A SPLINED SHAFT TO PROVIDE A MORE EFFICIENT SYSTEM WITH LESS TOLERANCE, WHILE ALSO PROVIDING SUBSTANTIAL WEIGHT SAVINGS. CRANKS ARE STATIC AND CANNOT BE ADJUSTED.

I DERAILLEURS: THE RESPECTIVE FUNCTIONS OF THE FRONT AND REAR DERAILLEURS ARE TO MOVE THE CHAIN FROM ONE SPROCKET OR CHAINRING ONTO THE NEXT.

Set-up and fit

A bike is like a suit. If it fits well, you enjoy wearing it because it makes you feel good. If you are uncomfortable, you will hate it. So, your first aim is to ascertain that the bike fits — and you will love riding it.

Derailleurs

Derailleurs offer a substantial amount of adjustment. Each derailleur comes equipped with two limiting screws, which can be set to limit the range in which the mechanism will be allowed to operate. The rear derailleur has a cable-tension adjuster — also known as

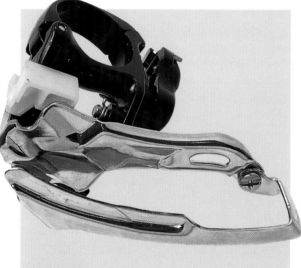

top FRONT DERAILLEUR

above REAR DERAILLEUR

a 'barrel adjuster' - which will increase the tension in the relevant cable when unscrewed (anti-clockwise), causing the derailleur to move the cable towards the larger sprocket, and to the next smaller sprocket if screwed inwards (clockwise).

Cranks

The primary interface for energy transfer between the rider and bike are the cranks. Not all cranks are equal, and prices may vary by as much as 400 per cent between entry-level and top-of-the-range equipment. Cranks on a mountain bike house up to three different sizes of chainring. This allows the rider to maintain a relatively high top speed on both downhills and flats, or to ride up very steep hills, depending on the selected gear ratio.

The configuration of these chainrings and the way they have been attached to the cranks may differ from crankset to crankset. Generally, they attach to the spindle via a tapered square hole in the crank, with a bolt holding the crank securely in position. Because they are static components, they cannot be adjusted — although chainrings may be swapped for different sizes within certain limits.

SHIMANO'S XTR CRANK

Gear shifters

Gear shifters should be set up comfortably so that you can operate them with ease. But, again, this is a matter of personal preference. Don't position them where you are able to make accidental shifts.

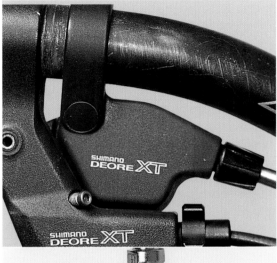

top SHIMANO'S XT RAPIDFIRE SHIFTERS

above A CAGED CLIPLESS PEDAL

you to disconnect or 'clip out' with a quick and simple outward twist of the heel — a much safer and easier option than that offered by the straps of toe clips. The only real adjustment you are able to make on clipless pedals is the spring tension, which can be set to determine the strength of the bond between shoe and pedal. Riders who are unfamiliar to this system may prefer to keep the spring tension a little slack initially.

Brakes

The feel, function and position of brakes will either inspire confidence or give you a rude awakening. The choice as to whether the rear brake should be activated by the left or right lever is entirely up to you, and there is no particular right or wrong way. However, be sure to remember which way around they are so that you do not inadvertently use the wrong brake and fly over the handlebars.

SHIMANO'S XTR 'V' BRAKES

Pedals

The toe clips on your pedals allow you to strap your feet to the pedal, resulting in better energy transfer. Clipless pedals require a pair of compatible shoes, which will allow you to install cleats under the sole, enabling you to be connected, or to 'clip' in, to the pedal. These, however, allow much less movement of the foot than the toe clips, but the system does enable

The position of the brake levers on the handlebars is important. These should not be horizontal, but positioned so that when your hands are on the grips in a normal riding position, and your middle fingers rest lightly on the levers, your wrists are straight. This will prevent injury to your wrists should you face an unexpected impact. The brunt of the impact is taken by your entire arm, and not just your wrists and hands.

Frame

The mountain bike frame should be considerably smaller than that you would choose for a road bike, simply because you need a lot more manoeuvrability on a mountain bike and may be hampered by too big a frame. The general rule is to select a mountain-bike frame about 8cm (3in) smaller than your road bike. The easiest way to determine the correct frame size is to straddle the bike, and stand flat footed over the top tube with the tip of the saddle just touching the small of your back. Now lift the front wheel off the ground so that the top tube touches your crotch. The front wheel should be 7 to 13cm off the ground. Do not compromise here. Rather make small adjustments in other areas to fine-tune the fit.

Saddles

The saddle can — and should be — adjusted to comfortably accommodate your height and build. To adjust the height of your saddle, have one friend hold the bike upright, while another stands behind you as you straddle the bike to check that your pelvis remains level. Position one of the pedals so that the crank arm is in line with the seat tube, pointing down. You should be able to touch the pedal with your heel when your leg is fully extended.

The saddle's position can also be fine-tuned, and experienced cyclists should be able to help. Most mountain bikers prefer the saddle to be positioned further back so that they have more leverage and are able to handle steeper descents.

ADJUST YOUR SADDLE HEIGHT TO ENSURE THAT YOUR PELVIS REMAINS LEVEL AS YOU STRADDLE THE BIKE.

EXAMPLES OF THE NEW ERGONOMIC SADDLE DESIGNS FOR BOTH WOMEN (TOP) AND MEN (ABOVE).

Stems and handlebars

The length of the stem and its 'rise' can be altered. Longer stems can lengthen the 'cockpit' of a bike, or shrink a 'cockpit' that feels too long. By lengthening the stem, you move a larger percentage of your body weight over the front wheel. This means that you will, on steep gradients, crash over the bars a lot quicker. In the days of flat bars, stem rises were used to raise the handlebar. With riser bars, a lower rise stem can be used. Bar-end extensions enhance your ability to transfer power, and give you more hand-position options.

HANDLEBARS ARE ATTACHED TO THE FRAME WITH A STEM AND HEADSET.

FOR A NOVICE, CYCLE SHOPS MAY APPEAR DAUNTING IN THEIR RANGE OF BICYCLES AND CYCLING GEAR, BUT SHOP ASSISTANTS ARE USUALLY KNOWLEDGEABLE AND ENTHUSIASTIC.

Manufacturers

Most quality brand-name bikes will come with a lifetime warranty on the frame for the first owner, so be sure to keep the original documentation and the serial number.

Mail order and on the Internet

If convenience is what you're after, or you live in a remote location where there are few cycle-related amenities, then this is an excellent option for you. Unfortunately, however, there is no personal interface with the salesperson, and you have no one to 'mentor' or advise you. The biggest problem is that complications may arise if something goes wrong.

Cycle shops

If the atmosphere in a cycle shop seems intimidating, walk straight out and find a shop that is friendly and supportive. If you buy a bike from a shop, the first service or two is usually free and they often throw in a few accessories as part of the deal. Cycle shops are usually run by enthusiasts, and the enthusiasm is bound to rub off on you.

Supermarkets

Merchandise buyers at super-markets concentrate on the mass market, and their aim is to move vast amounts of stock quickly. As such, neither your needs nor the bike you buy will have been given much attention. Just pull it off the rack, wheel it through the tills and its yours — for better or for worse.

THE MOST IMPORTANT CRITERION WHEN SHOPPING FOR A BIKE IS WHAT IT WILL BE USED FOR. A YOUNG NOVICE, FOR EXAMPLE, WILL NOT NEED A TOP-OF-THE-RANGE BIKE, WHICH HE OR SHE WILL OUTGROW BEFORE IT CAN BE APPRECIATED.

Essential accessories

The comfort and practicality of your cycle clothing will contribute to your enjoyment of mountain biking.

Cycling shorts

Proper cycling shorts offer additional comfort and protection in the form of padding in the crotch area, while the tight-fitting lycra fabric will prevent chafing and bunching against the saddle. When shopping for shorts, buy quality. Be wary of shorts with genuine leather chamois in the crotch as these will require extra care to prevent the leather from drying out. Synthetic chamois is much more convenient, works just as well, and can be washed in a standard washing machine. Shorts are also available in a 'bib' configuration, and these are often preferred by mountain bikers because they do not snag on the saddle or creep down while you ride. If you cycle for recreation, then consider buying a pair of ordinary, pocketed shorts with a netted inner lining that is padded.

cold when wet, and vice versa. Of course, if the cost is not an issue, then you may want to consider a GoreTex™ jacket, which is not only light-weight and waterproof, but also tear resistant.

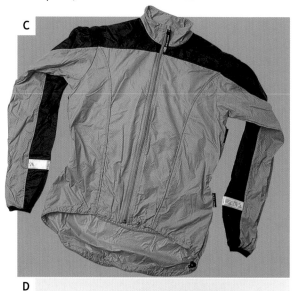

A LYCRA SHORTS OFFER COMFORT AND PREVENT CHAFING IN THE SEAT.

B SOME 'BAGGIES' HAVE TIGHT-FITTING, PADDED INNER SHORTS.

C A CYCLING JACKET WILL HELP KEEP OUT THE COLD AND WIND.

D CYCLING JERSEYS MAY BE LONG- OR SHORT-SLEEVED.

Jackets

Cycling jackets perform the same function as a pullover or jersey, but are used to create an additional layer in very cold and/or wet conditions. It is best to keep a warm jacket and a rain jacket — especially when cycling long distances — since it is not always

Jerseys

Cycling jerseys will keep you warm and dry, and offer convenient pockets at the back in which to pack items you need to carry with you. Apart from functionality, bright colours make you more visible, although jerseys for recreational riders are often in subtle colours.

The perfect fit

'If the cycling craze of the 1890s restructured consumer demand in subtle ways, it fundamentally reformed social relations, in particular relations between the sexes.

The adjustment lay as much in the greater mobility gained by women, as in their newly acquired freedom from the constraints of fashion. The bicycle did more than just change the idea of female beauty ... it redefined women's social and political roles as well.'

The Bicycle,
by Pryor Dodge
(Flammarion, Paris, 1996)

DUE TO SOCIAL CONSTRAINTS, FEMALE RIDERS WERE FEW IN THE EARLY DAYS OF CYCLING. WESTERN SOCIETY HAS, HOWEVER, SEEN A GROWING INTEREST IN OFF-ROAD CYCLING AMONG WOMEN.

Frame geometry

Because women generally have longer legs and shorter torsos than men, the standard frame geometry of a bicycle may often result in some measure of discomfort for women, and many feel that they often have to 'stretch out' simply to accommodate the frame of the bike. There are, however, options that may make a female rider a little more comfortable. Fitting a shorter stem or riser bars may add to a woman's comfort, but it is best to look for a brand of bike that feels comfortable the moment you climb onto it.

Saddle position

Ideally, female riders should ensure that the nose of the saddle remains level, although some riders may even favour tilting it slightly down.

Saddle specifics

Women usually have wider hips than men, and now that more women are cycling, there are several woman-specific saddles from which to choose. A woman's saddle should only place pressure on the sit bones, and not on the genital area. Look at what is on the market to suit a woman's needs.

What to wear

Apart from a comfortable sports bra that will offer good support and keep the breasts firmly in place, female riders should also buy women's cycling shorts, as men's hips are narrower — and so is the padding.

The padding on men's cycling shorts will thus lie at the point on a woman's buttocks where she experiences the most pressure, and will in all probability cut into the flesh. Women's shorts, however, have a wider padding and will fit snugly around the waist to accommodate the female form.

Glasses

Much more than just a fashion accessory, a good pair of cycling glasses qualifies as protective eyewear against wind, sand, branches, and insects, while filtering out harmful ultraviolet and infrared radiation. A good pair of glasses should be as optically perfect as possible, while at the same time provide a shatter-resistant shield. Light weight, a comfortable fit, and a choice of lenses for different light conditions are important advantages. Consider purchasing a string to hang them around your neck, so that you won't lose them in a fall. You may also need to remove your glasses while you are riding, especially when your vision is obscured by mud or the lenses mist up when it is cold.

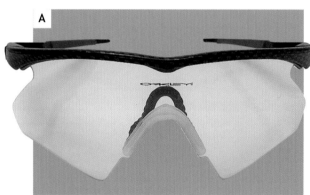

A

B

Shoes

Apart from training, perhaps the single most important thing you can do to improve your performance on the bike is to invest in a good pair of mountain-bike shoes. The snug fit and stiff sole will help you transfer maximum power into the drive-train, and you won't lose energy and feel discomfort from the flexing of the sole associated with sneakers. By combining a pair of SPD (Shimano Pedalling Dynamics) or similarly compatible shoes with proper clipless pedals, you will have the best of both worlds. Proper mountain-bike shoes should last at least a season or two under fairly hard racing conditions and, in fact, for several years when in casual use. Unlike road-cycling shoes, they are designed to be used for both riding and short stretches of walking — especially important in mountain biking, when you often have to dismount and carry the bike.

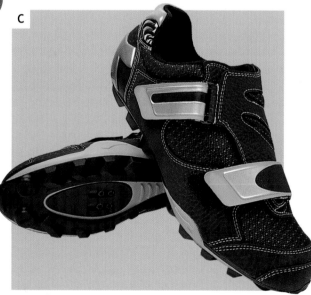

C

Gloves

A good pair of gloves is next in terms of importance and will ensure a proper grip on the handlebars under almost all weather and terrain conditions, offering protection from blistering and comfort for your hands. During a fall, your hands hit the ground first, so gloves will protect the skin and prevent serious abrasions. Long-finger, winter gloves will help prevent your hands cramping in the cold.

A LIGHTWEIGHT GLASSES ARE ESSENTIAL PROTECTIVE GEAR.

B RIDERS MAY CHOOSE FULL-FINGER OR HALF-FINGER GLOVES.

C MODERN MOUNTAIN-BIKING SHOES WITH A CLEAT-COMPATIBLE SOLE.

Helmet

A helmet is the most important accessory you will ever buy. Not only can it save your life, but without a helmet you will be refused participation in organized events. In order for a helmet to offer maximum protection, it should fit properly. The straps and padding need to be adjusted so that the helmet fits snugly on your head. Ensure that the model you choose has been certified by an accepted safety organization and carries a recognized certification mark.

Hydration systems

Even a small loss of your body's water content may seriously affect your performance. Rehydration during any form of exertion is of the utmost importance. Although water bottles work well, they are often difficult to use while riding off road. Your water bottle may come out of the cage or, worse still, the nozzle can become coated with mud. Because drinking may be difficult when you are in the saddle, you may not take in enough fluid, and this can cause loss of energy and, at worse, heat exhaustion. A hands-free drinking system worn as a backpack (such as the CamelBak™) will allow you to drink with ease while riding, and will help you to stay hydrated even when cycling at high speed or over rough terrain. Most modern versions of these systems have an outer pack that offers additional compartments to store food, tools, money, and the like. This is one accessory that is worth every penny.

Pumps

A foot or 'track' pump will help to inflate your tyres effortlessly and the pressure gauge will ensure you inflate them accurately. There are many good, mini 'double-shot' pumps on the market – but conventional bicycle pumps fit snugly onto your frame. However, it is important that your pump is either zipped safely away in a tool bag, or tightly secured onto your frame. The jolting and jarring of mountain biking often causes a pump to work its way loose and fall by the wayside.

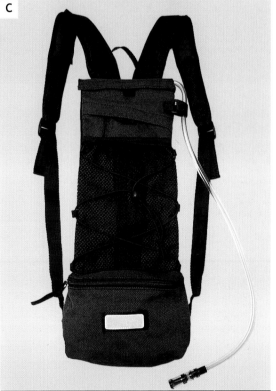

A A GENERAL RECREATIONAL RIDING/CROSS-COUNTRY HELMET

B TWO VARIETIES OF MINI HAND-PUMP

C HYDRATION SYSTEM

Mountain-bike applications

Before you buy a bike, decide what you want to do with it. One of the most important factors of the mountain bike is its versatility. They can be adapted for many applications, from recreation to racing, from law enforcement to transport and social empowerment.

Cycle touring

Mountain bikes make excellent touring machines, and this is largely due to their comfortable riding position and sturdy construction. Most mountain-bike frames have fittings for the attachment of panniers. However, remember that when touring in so-called Third World countries, spares may be hard to come by and an aluminium or exotic alloy frame may be difficult to fix. It is probably best to stick to steel, and to rid your bike of suspension or anything else that is superfluous and may take strain. Simplicity is the key. Remember that you cannot claim on your warranty with local agents when travelling in remote locations. It may be overkill but, with the additional weight of your baggage, some cycle tourists have avoided wheel failure by replacing the existing rims and hubs with tandem equipment.

Recreation

Most entry-level to middle-range mountain bikes are suitable for recreation. A fairly light bike with some sort of front suspension and an ordinary componentry groupset will provide many hours of carefree riding. However, do not try to race a cheap bike with weak components too often, as it is not designed for demanding terrain, and is best used for light trail riding, fitness training, commuting, or biking with the family.

TRUE TO THE VERY NAME OF THIS ADVENTURE SPORT, UNSPOILT MOUNTAINOUS TERRAIN REMAINS THE ULTIMATE CHALLENGE FOR MOUNTAIN BIKERS ACROSS THE GLOBE, AND IN FEW PLACES IS THE PROSPECT MORE EXHILARATING THAN IN THE SNOW-CAPPED PEAKS OF THE SWISS ALPS.

MUCH OF THE INNOVATION AND DEVELOPMENT IN MODERN BICYCLE TECHNOLOGY ORIGINATED ON THE RACE TRACK, WHICH MAKES SPECIFIC DEMANDS ON BOTH THE BIKE AND THE RIDER.

Competition

Competitive cycling is the testing ground for new technology, which will eventually find its way from top-end racing bicycles into most mass-market models. In fact, mountain-bike racing has gained so much popularity that the sport has now developed into multiple disciplines, with cross-country being awarded full medal status at the 1996 Olympic Games in Atlanta and Sydney 2000.

Today, of course, there are all sorts of disciplines for competitive racers, from cross-country to downhill racing, slalom and trials to long-distance endurance races. See also pages 38—40.

Commuting

A mountain bike is perfect for commuting. It offers more places to fit pannier racks. The heavier, stronger wheels will survive inner-city road debris and pothole-infested roads far better than a traditional road bike. The riding position also makes you more visible to traffic — and more stable on the bike — and it is therefore safer. The user-friendly gear ratios and brakes will help you manage the hills, and the stops and starts you will encounter in the uncontrolled cycling environment of the big city.

Adventure riding

Also known as 'free-riding', adventure riding is a combination of cross-country, or trail riding, and downhilling — and a whole new range of bikes has evolved from this. The idea is to ride on trails that challenge both your technical bike-handling skills and your level of fitness. The bikes used for adventure riding usually have dual-suspension, reinforced frames with disk brakes. They are heavier than cross-country bikes, and are designed to be ridden for long periods over rough terrain at high speed.

AN ENTIRE NEW RANGE OF BIKES HAS EVOLVED FOR FREE-RIDING.

Basic Riding Skills

many newcomers to the sport have a 'ride-from-hell' story to tell about their first experience of mountain biking. For many novices, the last time they rode a bicycle they were little more than toddlers and, as adults, they have to re-learn how to ride a bike! Get to know your new mountain bike — its shifters, gears, pedals — at a quiet car park or community centre where there is no traffic. Novices, anxious to move on to the new challenges that await, often make mistakes, which can erode their confidence. Simple mistakes include:

■ riding with mountain-bike clubs, friends or spouses who are not supportive and do not encourage you

■ tackling a technical trail beyond your current bike-handling skills and thus injuring yourself

■ entering in the wrong category or over the wrong distance in a race.

above OFTEN, AS ADULTS, WE HAVE TO RE-LEARN THE SKILLS THAT CAME SO EASY AS CHILDREN — LIKE RIDING A BICYCLE, FOR EXAMPLE.

opposite OFF-ROAD CYCLING OFFERS THE OPPORTUNITY TO EXPERIMENT WITH GEARS WHILE COVERING ADVENTUROUS TERRAIN AND GRADIENTS.

Handling hints

■ Don't be hypnotized into following the rider in front, or you may hit the obstacle they so effectively avoided! Keep your eyes on the trail ahead, not on your front wheel or the back wheel of the rider ahead of you.

■ When you hit an unexpected stretch of sand, mud or water, shift your weight off the front wheel by moving your weight to the back of the saddle. Do not brake sharply or stiffen your body or you will lose control. Spin through the obstacle in an easy gear, allowing the front wheel to 'float' over the unstable terrain.

■ Remember to feed and hydrate yourself regularly. Once every 20 minutes is ideal. If you don't do this, you will either 'bonk' or suffer from dehydration.

■ If you are going down a steep bank or riding downhill, always slide your weight back off the saddle. Should you lose control, it is far safer to fall off the back of your bike than to go headfirst over the bars!

■ Rather than focusing on the object you are trying to avoid on the trail, keep your eye focused ahead of you.

■ When riding up or down an incline, choose your line and commit to it. If you hesitate halfway down or up, you are sure to fall.

CYCLE IN A GROUP — IT IS FAR SAFER, AND YOU CAN LEARN A LOT FROM EXPERIENCED ENTHUSIASTS.

Enjoying the experience

Here are some guidelines to make your mountain-biking experience an enjoyable one:

Never ride off-road alone

Cycle in a group — it is safer, more social and offers some support for the beginner. You can learn a lot from fellow enthusiasts. Besides, other riders like sharing their routes and experiences with an enthusiastic novice. Make a point of establishing contact with mountain-bike clubs in your area, and other clubs or organisations which may organise cycling excursions.

Talk to the contact person

Organised mountain-bike rides should be graded to help you decide which will best suit your needs and level of competence. If they are not, ask the contact person what the distances are, the expected time they will

take to complete, and whether there is a slow group and/or sweep riders. A novice rider should, ideally, not attempt an off-road ride of more than 15km/9 miles.

Be prepared

Eat and drink some two hours before you leave for a ride. Your body is sure to burn up energy and fluid on the ride, so it is important that you feed and hydrate it to replenish lost resources. Try not to eat a rich meal — one that is fatty or has a rich sauce — or drink alcohol, as you may suffer from indigestion and nausea on the ride. Ensure, too, that your bicycle is in good working condition, and that you have a spare tube and a pump. You do not drive a car without a spare wheel — so the same should apply to your cycling.

Before you start

■ Apply sunblock. If you have scars, pay particular attention to them, as this sensitive skin is the most vulnerable to skin cancer.

■ When you offload your bike, tighten all the wheel skewers properly, and make sure that the levers are twisted away so they do not snag on vegetation.

BE PREPARED! WHEN PLANNING AN EXCURSION, BE SURE TO TAKE YOUR OWN WATER AND OTHER ESSENTIALS FOR A COMFORTABLE RIDE.

■ Connect your brakes if you have disconnected the wheels for transportation. If they rub against your wheel, check that the wheel has been properly inserted, and tighten again.

■ Check that your saddle is at the correct height.

■ Introduce yourself to the ride organizer. If it is a ride organized by a club, you may be required to sign an indemnity and pay a small fee.

■ Stretch your muscles before or during the pre-ride briefing to warn your body that it is to be exerted.

Let the adventure begin

Relax and enjoy! As the pack gets going, do not be tempted to ride too fast, too soon. Allow 10 minutes to warm up. Set your own pace, and while you are admiring the scenery, make a mental note of landmarks — just in case you lose your way later on. If this is your first ride, be sure to experiment with the wide variety of gears rather than grinding away in one gear, wearing yourself out. You will encounter all sorts of different gradients and surfaces. The wide range of gear ratios on your mountain bike is designed for the challenges this presents the rider. Watch and talk to the other cyclists and heed their advice. If the route crosses any main roads where there is traffic, keep your wits about you. Many riders are so relaxed during an off-road ride that they even forget to look left and right when they are crossing a road. If the road is very busy, rather dismount and walk your bike across.

Reward yourself

On the way home, stop for tea and cake at a café or coffee shop to reward yourself. Try not to arrange anything too demanding after a mountain-bike ride, because you will, in all likelihood, be too tired to enjoy much! Be kind to your body when you have finished cycling: don't forget to stretch your muscles again (just as you did at the start), and put on something warm after a ride. Your shirt will be wet with sweat, and your body temperature drops as soon as you stop exercising (ideal conditions to catch a cold). Now go home and enjoy a good rest — it is just as important as riding.

Important controls

A bike's most important controls are the pedals, handlebars, gear shifters, brake levers and saddle.

■ Without even realizing it, you often use the saddle as a lever for control by pushing the bike with your inner thighs to achieve the correct lean angle. Try to ride without it, and you will understand why!

■ The brake system should be set up so that you can lock a brake simply by using the middle finger of each hand. The tilt of the lever should be such that your wrists are straight and form an extension of your arm when your fingers are resting on the brake lever. Most important is that you should know exactly which lever controls the front brake, and which lever the rear, without having to think about it. This is important because you will not have time to consider this in an emergency or a tricky technical section — and accidentally using the front brake when you mean to use the rear can send you flying off the bike.

■ Gear shifters should function flawlessly on both upshifts and downshifts. This is an important element when you are trying to get out of trouble or performing certain manoeuvres on the bike. If shifting problems exist, get the shop assistants to replace the cables or adjust the tension.

■ Pedals should be in a good condition, since these are your main contact with the bike — apart from the handlebars and saddle — and are your direct medium for energy transfer. If you are using clipless pedals, your shoes should also be in a good condition, and the pedals should release the cleat easily when you try to 'clip out'.

■ Grips should be of a diameter that may be easily handled by your size of hands. These should be hard or soft, depending on your hands' sensitivity to pressure.

■ Bar-end extensions (when fitted) should be positioned at a safe angle, while at the same time enhancing the geometry, and providing additional handlebar grip positions. This is particularly useful when you need additional power in climbing or extra comfort.

YOUR LEGS DO MOST OF THE WORK — EVEN WHEN YOU HAVE MASTERED
ADVANCED TECHNIQUES — SO BE SURE TO STRETCH YOUR LEG MUSCLES.

Down to the nitty gritty

With your maiden ride behind you, it is time to prepare for more advanced cycling.

The fit and set-up of your bike

To successfully control your bike, it has to be of a size and fit that complements your body dimensions and ability. It is thus important to choose the correct frame size (see page 16), and find the correct saddle height (see page 16). If you feel cramped or stretched out on the bike, then replace the existing stem with a longer or shorter model. Altering stem length will change the bike's handling characteristics, and you should get used to this before riding trails. A short stem means that you carry less weight on the front wheel, resulting in loose traction at the front when cornering at high speed. You will have to compensate by placing more weight over the front wheel. A longer stem may limit your ability to handle steep drop-offs, and you will be more likely to fly over the handlebars. Brake levers, gear shifters, bar ends, handlebars and grips should be set up to enhance handling and provide comfort.

Warming up and cooling down

Most cyclists neglect to warm up or stretch their muscles, and this can result in both injury and poor performance. Cycling is primarily a cardiovascular endurance sport, so warming up prepares muscles and sinews, leaving them ready for action. Stretching first, then riding at low intensity and gradually increasing it, will help your body change from anaerobic to aerobic at a gentler pace. After the ride, the same applies, but in reverse: slow down from high intensity to lower intensity, and finish with a stretching session.

Hand position

Hand position is dictated by your own preference, but some guidelines may help keep you out of trouble.
■ Never grip the bars too tightly. This will cause your upper body to tense up, which can result in a loss of control, as well as tire your hands and arms.
■ Never place your thumb on the top of the bar with your other fingers while riding. If you should hit an unexpected obstacle, your hands will slip off the bar.
■ Hold your hands loosely on the bar. Elbows should be slightly bent and your shoulders relaxed, not hunched.

Braking

You need no more than one or two fingers to apply enough force on the levers to lock the wheels. You should never need to use all four fingers to activate your brakes, because you need your other three fingers to maintain a secure grip to control the bike and brake at the same time. Front brakes offer better braking performance than the rear brake. Depending on the terrain and braking power, however, they should still be used with discretion. Unless you have developed sufficient skill, never use the front brakes during short, extreme descents, or during high-speed cornering on loose terrain. During long descents, do not keep the brakes on continuously as this will heat the rim and brake pads so that they 'glaze over', diminishing their stopping power. 'Feather' the brakes by applying and relaxing the brakes until you reach the bottom. This will help reduce the build-up of heat, and you will still maintain your braking power and control of the bike.

Pedalling technique

Since the pedals transfer energy, develop a technique that will help achieve maximum energy transfer.

■ Proper cycling shoes and clipless pedals will help.

■ Cranks revolve around a central spindle and the pedals thus follow a circular path.

■ To provide a smooth and constant delivery of power to the drive-train, you have to learn to consistently pedal in circles, instead of mashing the pedals up and down. The best way to learn the correct technique is to ride on smooth terrain or on the road, concentrating on the four phases (*below*) of the pedal stroke.

■ It is generally accepted that a high 'cadence' — pedal rotations per minute (RPM) — is more energy efficient, hence the explosion in the popularity of 'spinning'. However, when riding off-road it is virtually impossible to maintain any rhythm at all, let alone a high cadence. The only exception is when you are riding a quality full-suspension bike, which allows you to sit down more often, thereby allowing you to maintain a higher cadence.

■ Remember to check yourself regularly (or ask another rider or a knowledgeable instructor at your training institute) and adjust your pedalling technique if you find that you are mashing down on the pedals, rather than spinning.

Weight distribution

When properly positioned on the bike, standing on a flat surface, you should have roughly 60 per cent of your weight over the rear wheel and 40 per cent over the front. This distribution allows enough flexibility to climb steep inclines without the bike flipping over backwards, and to descend down steep sections without flying over the bars.

■ **Descending** Always keep your weight back — even as far as placing your chest on the saddle if the gradient demands it.

■ **Climbing** Shift your weight to the back of the saddle to give your legs more leverage, while keeping your upper body low, crouching over the handlebars to 'bed in' the bike.

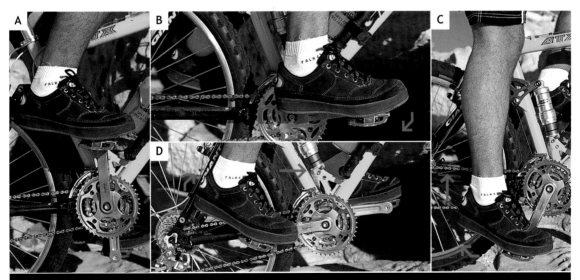

A PHASE 1 *DOWNWARD:* PUSH THE PEDAL DOWN, WITH EITHER YOUR TOES OR ANKLE LEADING. YOU WILL USUALLY HAVE MORE POWER IF YOUR ANKLE LEADS YOUR DOWNWARD THRUST, WITH YOUR HEEL POINTING DOWNWARDS AND TOES UPWARDS.

B PHASE 2 *BACKWARD:* DURING THIS PHASE, YOUR FOOT WILL TRAVEL ALONG THE BOTTOM OF THE STROKE, MOVING BACKWARDS. HERE YOU SHOULD ACTIVELY PULL YOUR FOOT BACK (AS IF YOU ARE SCRAPING MUD OFF THE BOTTOM OF YOUR SHOE).

C PHASE 3 *UPWARD:* HERE YOU SHOULD PULL UPWARDS ON THE PEDAL AS HARD AS YOU CAN HANDLE FOR A LONG PERIOD.

D PHASE 4 *FORWARD:* SIMPLY PUSHING THE PEDAL FORWARD WITH YOUR FOOT IS THE KEY OPERATION HERE.

Making sense of gears

Mountain bikes are equipped with gear ratios that will help achieve relatively high top speeds, with superior low-gear ratios to ride steep climbs. To make good use of them, you need to understand how they work.

In the middle of frame, bolted onto the cranks through the bottom bracket, are three chain rings. The sizes of these can vary: a big ring (48 to 42 teeth), a middle ring (36 to 32 teeth) and a small or 'granny ring' (26 to 20 teeth). At the back of the frame, centred around the hub of the back wheel, is a 'cluster' of sprockets with 36 to 11 teeth. Choosing a front ring with a specific rear sprocket, will result in a situation where, for one revolution of your legs, you will achieve a different number of revolutions for the rear wheel.

Example 1

You are riding in the biggest ring at the front (a 42-tooth ring) and the smallest sprocket at the back (an 11-tooth ring): 42 ÷ 11 = 3.8. For every revolution of your legs, the rear wheel would have rotated 3.8 times. This is usually the most difficult gear to ride, and is best for downhills.

Example 2

You are in the smallest ring at the front (a 22-tooth) and the largest sprocket at the back (a 32-tooth): 22 ÷ 32 = 0.68. For every leg revolution, the rear wheel will do just over half a revolution. This will be the easiest, or 'slowest' gear and is best for steep climbs.

Shifting gears

■ Don't perform gear shifts while the drive-train is fully loaded (when applying full pressure to the pedals). Back off the pressure momentarily while the shift completes.

■ Shift the gears in small increments rather than jump from one extreme to the other in a single shift.

■ Don't 'cross over' the chain. Avoid gear ratios that cause the chain to sit diagonally. The chain is 'crossed' when on the two largest sprockets at the back and the big chainring in the front, or the two smallest sprockets at the back while the chain is on the smallest chainring in the front.

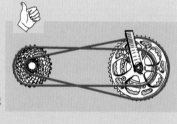

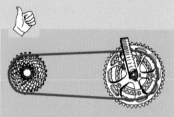

■ When the chain is on the middle chainring at the front, you may use the sprocket range of at the back.

EXAMPLE 1

EXAMPLE 2

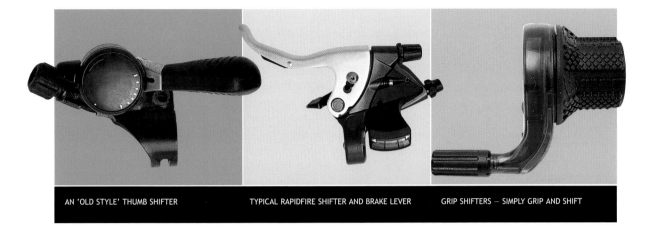

AN 'OLD STYLE' THUMB SHIFTER   TYPICAL RAPIDFIRE SHIFTER AND BRAKE LEVER   GRIP SHIFTERS — SIMPLY GRIP AND SHIFT

Shifting systems

Mountain bikes have a front derailleur, activated by a shifter on the left side of the handlebar, and a rear derailleur activated by a shifter on the right. Derailleurs move the chain from one sprocket to the next.

■ **Thumb shifters** These simple shifters were bolted to the top of the handlebars, and were activated by pushing the lever with the thumb and forefinger.

■ **RapidFire shifters** These are usually located beneath the handlebars, and are operated by two push-buttons (on older models) or a push-and-pull lever (on modern versions). Back shifters can shift down (into an easier gear) one to three gears at a time, but shift up only one gear at a time. Front shifters can shift one gear at a time in both directions. Some models have a small visual indicator to show the gears you have selected.

■ **Grip Shifters** These shifters rotate around the handlebar, as opposed to rotating around their own pivot bolted onto the handlebar. Grip Shifters form part of the handlebar grip, and allow you to twist a portion of the handlebar grip (like a motorcycle throttle), thus activating the derailleurs. The term Grip Shift belongs to the SRAM Corporation, but there are other makes.

Shifting techniques

Always anticipate the terrain ahead and shift well in advance. Although the quality and operation of bicycle drive-trains have improved over the last few years and shifts can be made under pressure, it is best to release pressure on the chain momentarily to allow a smooth transition. Ignoring this rule could result in damaged chains, bent chainrings and teeth, and failing gears.

The chain

The roller-chain is an advanced and highly engineered piece of machinery. Specially chamfered side plates allow easy shifting and silent operation, while new alloys provide a balance between hardness and strength. A well-lubricated chain provides about 96 per cent efficiency in energy transfer, while the average vehicle transmission is only about 85 per cent efficient. To perform well, the chain must be clean and lubricated. Be sure to clean your chain regularly with environment-friendly degreaser, and lubricate before every ride with a proper bicycle chain lubricant (available from most bike shops). Avoid lubricating the chain with household or engine oil. This will attract dust and sand and, apart from leaving oily black marks everywhere, it will also shorten the life span of your drive-train.

THE BICYCLE CHAIN IS STILL THE MOST EFFICIENT TYPE OF DRIVE-TRAIN.

THE SURFACE OF HARD-PACK TERRAIN MAY BE A LIKE A TARRED ROAD.

Conquering the terrain

Much of the challenge of cycling off-road is being able to handle the bike over a variety of terrain conditions.

Hard-pack terrain

Hard-pack surfaces are the easiest and most comfortable to ride. Because this terrain is like a paved road — and even, on occasion, offers a better surface — the lack of rolling resistance may allow rapid progress. But remember that hard-pack terrain can be slippery when wet or covered by gravel or leaves.

Rocky terrain

Rocky terrain can be intimidating because the rocks throw you off balance and make it difficult to steer. Honing your technical skills, staying relaxed on the bike and learning to 'pick a line' are key here. The best way to ride rocky ground is to go with the flow — as if you were surfing.

Going down Depending on the nature of the trail, taking the risk of greater speed and momentum will often get you through a rocky section. The faster you go, the smoother it becomes. You will, however, need to 'read' the terrain over which you are riding.

Going up Don't bother being in the saddle on a rocky trail — you will inevitably be thrown about. If it is a short section, stand up out of the saddle in a crouched position over the handlebars (to keep your centre of gravity low), and the bike bedded in. This way, you will have more agility to counter-balance the bike, more leverage with your legs, and more control over the front wheel. Dropping your elbows will help keep the front wheel from lifting.

OBSTACLES WILL AFFECT THE BALANCE, LEVERAGE AND CONTROL YOU HAVE OVER YOUR MOUNTAIN BIKE.

Climbing

The mantra for climbing is: 'It's not how you start, it's how you finish.' Since 'mountain' is part of the term 'mountain bike,' climbs are inevitable — but so are downhills, of course!

Short, steep hills

These hills are climbed at high intensity. The duration of effort is short and intense, but position is crucial. Build up momentum during the run up to help carry you to the top. Steep climbs often start after a tight corner, which means that you have no momentum, but the challenge is to maintain traction. The idea is to find a position that allows you to keep enough weight over the rear wheel, but also enough over the front wheel so that the bike does not flip.

Long hills

Long hills do not require the same intensity and handling skills as steep climbs, but stick to a few rules.

■ Find a comfortable position, which you are able to maintain for the duration of the climb (3–30 minutes).

■ Start at a pace you are able to maintain. Start slowly and in an easy gear. You can always increase your speed later and shift to a more challenging gear, which will allow you to accelerate up and over the hill.

IF YOU START CLIMBING LONG HILLS AT A PACE YOU ARE UNABLE TO KEEP UP THROUGHOUT THE CLIMB, YOU WILL FIND THAT YOU 'BURN OUT' RATHER QUICKLY.

■ Shift your weight back on the saddle so that your legs have more leverage on the pedals.

■ Keep your upper body relaxed so that you can transfer energy and focus on climbing.

IF YOU ENCOUNTER EXTENDED SECTIONS OF A TRAIL THAT ARE BOUND TO HAMPER YOUR RIDE, RATHER CARRY YOUR BIKE THAN RISK DAMAGING IT.

Sand

Long stretches of sand are often impassable, and your bike will have to be carried, but short sections of sand attacked at speed can be traversed successfully.

When approaching a sandy patch, gather enough speed before you reach it. Before you actually hit the sand, shift down by one or two gears and move your weight back, so that your front wheel is 'light' and does not dig in. Keep the pedals spinning smoothly with enough power to maintain your speed, and do not 'steer' by turning the handlebars. The idea here is to skim over the sand as quickly as possible, without getting bogged down. When you encounter patches of sand on a track, you can often ride on the edges of the trail, where the terrain is firmer. Wet or damp sand can often be crossed without too much of a problem, as long as weight is kept off the front wheel and power is smoothly applied.

MOST SANDY PATCHES MAY BE CROSSED AT RELATIVELY HIGH SPEED.

Descending

The mantra of descending is: 'The faster you go, the smoother it becomes.'

Steep downhills or drop-offs

Keeping your weight far back will usually get you down an incline. Only use the front brake gently if the rear brake does not offer enough stopping power without locking up (it's best to not touch the front brake at all). You may have to move your weight back so far that your arms stretch out as far as they can and your chest is on the saddle (lower the saddle at the outset). It is safer to fall off the back than to fly over the front!

Dropping in or dropping off

'Dropping in' means going down with front wheel first, while 'dropping off' means wheelying off the edge and landing on the rear wheel. These advanced skills are covered in Chapter 4: Enhancing the Adventure.

Long, fast downhills

Although these are the most enjoyable downhills and never fail to provide an adrenaline rush when taken at speed, be very cautious if there are likely to be other users on the trail, and do not go beyond your own ability. Always wear a helmet and protective clothing when you are following a designated downhill route at speed, and avoid doing them alone. If you crash — or, literally, go over the edge — there will be someone to help you.

KEEP YOUR WEIGHT BACK IN ORDER TO HELP YOU SUCCESSFULLY NEGOTIATE A STEEP DROP-OFF.

LIKE MOST DESCENTS, LONG, FAST DOWNHILLS REQUIRE SOME ADVANCED SKILLS, BUT ALWAYS ERR ON THE SIDE OF CAUTION.

Mud

Unless you are willing to ride only in dry weather, be prepared to encounter muddy terrain virtually everywhere you go — what cannot be cured, must be endured! You have to accept that, on descents and climbs, you will slip a lot and carrying your bike is often the only option. Mud tends to collect on the frame where the wheel passes through, clogging up the works, and sticking to your tyres. Riding through water where available, will help wash away the mud and alleviate some of the problem. Try to avoid locking up the brakes since this will make you lose even more traction.

Riding in these conditions requires adaptations to your bicycle, and equipment- and bike-handling skills.
■ You will need to cover the chain with a lubricant designed to withstand wet, muddy conditions.
■ You will also have to fit tyres designed for muddy conditions that will offer firm traction.

RIDING OVER GRASS AND OTHER VEGETATION MEANS RIDING AGAINST RESISTANCE, MAKING THE TERRAIN PHYSICALLY DEMANDING.

■ If you use a clipless pedal system, then it needs to have ample mud clearance capabilities, or you will get locked in or out of your pedals. Some riders actually swap their clipless pedals for normal platform pedals, or toe clip pedals. Other riders use platform pedals with a built-in clip.
■ A bike equipped with disc brakes has an obvious advantage in these conditions over a bike equipped with standard cantilever or 'V' brakes.
■ Waterproof shoes will help keep your feet warm and dry — which are especially welcome on long rides.
■ Unless it is raining, stay away from plastic rain jackets. Choose clothing that breathes well.
■ Wash your bike thoroughly after every ride — especially if you have encountered stretches of mud.

Vegetation

Riding over thick vegetation — such as a carpet of leaves or pine needles on a forest floor, or even grass — causes resistance to the forward motion of your bike. Make sure that you do not send your heart rate soaring and exhaust yourself. You can also suffer from loss of traction, so treat this type of terrain the same way you would muddy ground.

IF YOU OFTEN ENCOUNTER MUD, CONSIDER MUD-SPECIFIC TYRES AND CHAIN LUBRICANTS — BUT NOTHING WILL GET YOU THROUGH A SWAMP.

Cornering

This is an area of bike handling in which everybody seems to struggle initially. However, once you have mastered the physical and psychological basics of cornering, you will be surprised at how fast and how low you can go without crashing.

Fast cornering

Fast cornering demands little more than determination and courage. The most instinctive habit to unlearn is the tendency to apply brakes in the corner. This not only places stress on the available traction, but the braking forces tend to flip the bike upright, and this makes it even more difficult to hold a line through the corner. The secret is

TRY TO ACCELERATE OUT OF A FAST CORNER RATHER THAN TO INSTINCTIVELY APPLY BRAKES.

to enter the corner at a speed with which you feel comfortable, accelerating out of it rather than having to brake in it. You need to choose a line and then stick to it — trying to bail out halfway through a corner is the worst thing you can do!

Cornering on loose terrain

Cornering on loose ground is not very different to fast cornering, except that you have even less traction and need to be more in control of your bike. Unclipping the inside foot and using it motocross-style as an outrigger to help stabilize when you lose traction can help prevent crashes, but needs to be practised in order to use this technique with some confidence.

LOOSE TERRAIN MEANS LESS CONTROL SO HANDLING TECHNIQUE NEEDS TO BE YOUR PRIORITY.

Enhancing the Adventure

no matter what your choice of cycling — racing, recreation, adventure, or simply commuting — mountain biking and off-road cycling is one sport that will seldom disappoint. Your enjoyment of the freedom and new discoveries it offers will continue to grow as you become more adventurous and capable.

The disciplines of racing

Little can compete with the exhilaration of a race, and mountain bikers may choose from an array of exciting disciplines that range from cross-country to endurance, downhill to dual slalom events. All these disciplines offer a challenge, and the opportunity to spend even more time on your mountain bike.

Cross-country racing

Cross-country racing is the most common discipline in mountain-bike racing, attracting the biggest fields of competitors — largely because these races cater for a wide range of cyclists, from children and beginners to enthusiasts and hardened experts.

Lap racing

Lap racing is the format followed by world championships and Olympic competition. The rules simply state that the rider must race around a marked route for a predetermined number of laps. During this time, the rider may only receive refreshments in the designated areas, and may accept no outside assistance whatsoever. All spare parts and tools must be carried by the cyclist, and mechanical repairs must be carried out by the rider. The rider must finish the race with the bike and wheels with which he or she started the race. The bike may be ridden, carried or pushed on the course, and riders must wear a helmet throughout the race. In fact, one of the main reasons for the continued growth of the sport is because there are so few of the stifling rules and regulations applicable to road cycling.

Long-distance endurance racing

Long-distance endurance racing is becoming more popular than lap racing. Instead of cycling laps around a short course, riders race around a wide loop or a long-distance point-to-point route. Some of the rules applicable to lap racing are ignored to accommodate this format: riders, for example, are permitted to receive refreshments at more than one point on the route and assistance from other competitors in the race is often allowed. Long-distance endurance racing is by far the most popular discipline among non-professional, or recreational racers since it is little more than a race against yourself.

above CROSS-COUNTRY RACING IS ONE OF THE MOST POPULAR DISCIPLINES.

opposite TRIALS RIDING IS AN EXTREME DISCIPLINE PRACTISED BY ONLY A FEW EXPERTS.

24-hour team or solo endurance events

These events are growing more popular every year. All the normal rules for lap racing apply — but usually in a team format. Teams or solo riders try to log as many laps as they can within 24 hours. Lights are used at night, and teams may schedule their own shifts.

Downhill racing

Downhill racing may be defined as a 'time trial', where riders start at an elevated point and follow a marked route to finish at a point of lower elevation. Courses are more extreme and bikes have met the challenge.

Timed runs

The timed run is the traditional form of downhill racing, and is based on the time the rider takes to complete the course. In some instances, the rider may be permitted to take two runs, and the faster of the two clocked times is recorded. Qualifying runs determine the starting positions, and the slower riders are permitted to start ahead of the faster riders.

Dual eliminators

In this downhill race, riders leave the start in pairs and race each other to the finish. The loser is eliminated, and the winner is paired with another winner until there are only two riders left. The victor in this race is the overall winner, and the loser takes second place.

Dual slalom

Reminiscent of MBX, this is raced over a shorter, artificial course, including jumps, hard corners, and a series of gates and poles to be negotiated. Each rider follows a set course or line and the elimination process is much the same as it is in dual eliminator downhills.

Duel

This is a combination of the dual eliminator and dual slalom. Riders start on separate lines, but these merge after the first corner, where the dual slalom-type race changes to an eliminator race. There are few rules and body contact is allowed while competitors 'duel' toward the finish.

24-HOUR EVENTS CAN BE BOTH CHALLENGING AND FUN, BUT RIDING UNDER THE COVER OF DARKNESS HAS DEMANDS OF ITS OWN.

DOWNHILL RACING REQUIRES GOOD HANDLING SKILLS AND PLENTY OF COURAGE, BUT FEW OTHER DISCIPLINES CAN MATCH THE THRILL.

KEEP THE BASICS IN MIND AND CRASHES WILL RESULT IN FEWER AND LESS SERIOUS INJURIES.

Quite apart from the pain and embarrassment of taking a tumble, there is no reason why you should fall if you take the right precautions. Most falls can be avoided — or the injuries minimised — if you keep in mind some simple rules.

■ **Stop the falling action as soon as possible.** Imagine you are cresting a hill and you are suddenly faced with a badly eroded and rutted slope, leading into a ditch filled with boulders. If you are heading down too fast and cannot stop in time, it may be better to throw yourself to the side while you are still near the top of the hill (and walk away with a few scratches and bruises) rather than career down into the ditch — and end up with far more serious injuries.

■ **Keep your limbs to yourself, tuck and tumble.** Although it is easier said than done when you are caught up in the panic, it is important that you do not stick out your arms and hands to prevent the fall. Limbs are easily injured this way. Keep your arms and legs close to your body, and allow your trunk to take the full impact. Tucking yourself into a ball (rather like you may have been taught in judo class) will allow you to escape with fewer injuries.

■ **Go with the momentum.** Do not fight the fall; simply go with the momentum and ride it out until it is all over. When you land, roll along the ground until you come to a stop. Skidding will simply tear and rip your tyres, and inevitably result in an injury. Of course, if you are sliding towards a cliff or steep mountainside, then skid by all means — and find something to break the skid and bring you to a stop.

■ **Allow the bike to absorb some impact.** Sometimes, it may be a good idea just to allow yourself to go down with the bike so that it can help cushion your fall. Damaged bike parts can be replaced — body parts cannot.

■ **Slip off the back of the bike.** If you are on a downhill or drop-off and you are about to fall and are going to have to bail, then simply abandon the bike by sliding off the back. The bike will eventually stop and, without your weight, it may not be damaged at all — and you will avoid a painful collision.

■ **Avoid falling directly on your shoulder.** Falling onto your shoulder is certain to result in a broken collarbone or worse. If you find yourself colliding with another object from the side, try to fall forward or backward where you are less likely to land on your shoulder.

Advanced skills

Crashes are as much a part of mountain biking as traffic congestion is to a motorist. It happens to everybody — even the professionals. Once you have made peace with this fact, you will be ready to face the serious challenges, and learn the more advanced skills.

THE BUNNY HOP: STEP 1 FOCUS ON THE OBSTACLE WELL BEFORE YOU REACH IT, AND APPROACH IT WITH REASONABLE SPEED. RELAX YOUR BODY IN ADVANCE AND BEND YOUR ARMS AND LEGS INTO A CROUCHING POSITION SO THAT YOU ARE HUDDLED OVER THE BIKE.

THE BUNNY HOP: STEP 2 BEFORE THE FRONT WHEEL MEETS THE OB-STACLE (50CM/2FT), COMPRESS THE FRONT OF THE BIKE BY PUSHING DOWNWARDS. LAUNCH YOURSELF UPWARDS AND FORWARD WITH AN EXPLOSIVE ACTION OF THE LEGS AND ARMS. PULL THE HANDLEBARS UP.

THE BUNNY HOP: STEP 3 AS THE FRONT WHEEL STARTS TO CLEAR THE OBSTACLE, START APPLYING A TWISTING FORCE ON THE HANDLEBARS AND PULL BACKWARDS AND UPWARDS WITH YOUR FEET (SPD PEDALS HELP HERE). THE REAR WHEEL SHOULD LEAVE THE GROUND AND FOLLOW THE PATH OF THE FRONT WHEEL.

THE BUNNY HOP: STEP 4 CHANGE THE CENTRE OF GRAVITY BY MOVING YOUR WEIGHT FORWARD OR BACKWARD. MOVING WEIGHT FORWARD WILL FORCE THE FRONT WHEEL DOWN; MOVING BACKWARD WILL RAISE THE FRONT WHEEL. THE AIM IS TO LAND ON THE REAR WHEEL FIRST AND THEN ALLOW THE SECOND WHEEL TO TOUCH DOWN.

The bunny hop

Jumping, or the bunny hop, can be used with great effect to overcome obstacles without interrupting your progress or losing speed. This jump is most often necessary when you have to clear an obstacle on a trail without the benefit of a ramp or lip to help launch you off the ground. The concept of the bunny hop is relatively simple and the key is to practise as often as possible. Start with small, easy obstructions in your path, and work your way over larger obstacles as your skill and confidence grow.

Jumping with a ramp

Much like the bunny hop, the key here is to relax on the bike. Start with jumps you feel you can handle, working on your own technique before progressing to more advanced skills.

Launching off a lip or ramp will allow you to jump quite a distance before touching down. There are, as with the bunny hop, three distinct phases: the approach, the jump, and the landing.

The approach Look well ahead, so you can see the jump well in advance. As you approach, relax and lower your body into the crouching position, bending your arms and legs.

The jump As you hit the jump, you need to stand up quickly because, as the bike is being forced upwards, it will push towards you. At this stage, bend your legs and arms again so that the bike can move up and towards you. At the same time, keep your weight back so that the saddle has space to move towards your stomach area. When you and the bike are airborne, push the bike away from you again, but keep your arms and legs slightly bent so that you are able to flex them during the landing.

The landing The landing can be defined in two phases: landing the bike, and landing the rider. Although it is not always possible, let the rear wheel touch down first, and then the front wheel. Once both wheels are on the ground, your own weight will also come down on the bike. Allow your extended arms and legs to bend and gradually transfer your full weight onto the bike. And you're down!

JUMPING WITH A RAMP: STEP 1 THE APPROACH

JUMPING WITH A RAMP: STEP 2 THE JUMP

JUMPING WITH A RAMP: STEP 3 THE LANDING

Climbing

Since mountain biking implies that you will be riding in the mountains, it follows that riding uphill is part of the experience. Apart from fitness and strength, the correct technique will greatly assist you in conquering almost any hilly trail. In order to keep going forward and upwards, two critical components need to be present: power and movement through the drive-train, and traction. Power and movement are directly related to strength and fitness. Traction is related to skill, the type of tyres on your bike, and the position of your weight and tyre pressure.

Steep hills, loose gravel and bad traction

The secret to maintaining a forward motion on these climbs lies in finding the perfect balance between weight distribution, posture, power, pedalling style, and the best line.

BODY POSITION, CONTROL AND POWER ARE KEY IN CONQUERING TECHNICAL CLIMBS.

STANDING STILL MAY CAUSE YOU TO LOSE TRACTION.

Weight distribution Most riders tend to stand on steep and difficult climbs. This works well on solid surfaces offering good traction but, in typical off-road conditions, circumstances are substantially different and technique starts to play an important role. Moving your weight backwards on the saddle will place more weight on the rear wheel, which will provide better traction but, unfortunately, will also cause the front wheel to lift, which will make the bike difficult to steer and will most probably cause the bike to flip over backwards. Moving your weight forward will keep the front wheel on the ground, but the rear wheel will spin in the loose ground and cause you to stall.

Posture Having considered all the criteria listed above, you will still need to make small adjustments and move your weight around as the terrain dictates. You may find yourself perching on the nose of the saddle to achieve the optimum distribution, so a good tip is to remember to keep your elbows below the level of the handlebar grips, as if you are trying to pull

CHOOSING THE BEST LINE IS KEY, AND COMES WITH EXPERIENCE.

Long climbs

All the general rules apply here too, but depend on the severity of the terrain and the gradient of the climb. However, since the climb may extend for quite a distance, it is important to pace yourself and pick a speed and gear ratio that is sustainable for the duration of the climb. To conquer most hills, you will need both fitness and strength, technique and the right attitude.

You may not be strong enough to conquer many hills initially but, with training and regular riding, you will soon improve. Try not to worry about the whole hill at once, but concentrate on small, manageable sections and complete those before embarking on the next. Also, keep in mind that it is more important to complete the climb than to worry about the time in which you do it. Once you are able to ride most climbs with confidence you can work on the element of speed.

DIFFICULT CLIMBS MAY REQUIRE YOU TO BEND YOUR BODY INTO ALL SORTS OF POSITIONS IN ORDER TO MAINTAIN TRACTION AND KEEP THE BIKE MOVING FORWARD.

the handlebars down. This will help keep the front wheel of the bike on the ground, even though it may not always be very comfortable.

Power and pedalling style In order to propel the bike forward, you need a smooth, constant output of power into the drive-train. If there is too much power, you will loose traction; too little power, and you will slow down or stall. Mashing the pedals up and down, instead of pedalling in smooth round circles will cause your wheel to spin out and you will lose traction.

Technical climbs

All the rules that apply to steep hills are applicable to technical climbs too – except that you will also have to contend with finding the correct line. You need to pick your way through the rocks, ruts and roots carefully. Scan the terrain about 5m/16ft ahead of your front wheel, and pick the best line to follow. But be sure to stick to the line you have chosen, and do not make any last-minute changes.

Restarting on steep, loose climbs

It is very difficult to start again after you have stalled and spun out on a climb. You may have to dismount to move back or forward a little to find a suitable starting position. Look for an area where the terrain is flatter, or where you can find good traction, like a rock sheet, for example. Choose a gear that is not too powerful but one you can still handle — too powerful a gear will cause you to stall again. Start with your preferred leg (the leg with which you usually start, and often your stronger leg) and with your brakes engaged. Now apply the power, and gently let go of the brakes. The moment the bike starts moving forward, put the other foot on the other pedal and pedal smoothly, accelerating until you are back on track. Another good technique is to park the bike diagonally across the trail, and then turn up the trail the moment you get going.

LEARNING HOW TO RESTART SMOOTHLY ON STEEP CLIMBS WILL HELP YOU KEEP A CONSISTENT PACE THROUGHOUT THE RIDE.

Downhills

Keep your body relaxed. Riding with stiff arms and legs will not only shake you around, but the bike will bounce over the trail. A crouched position, with the legs and elbows slightly bent and your backside resting only lightly on the saddle, will help you to achieve a faster ride with a lot more comfort and control. Keeping your body weight slightly back and behind the saddle will also allow more space for the frame to move and thus absorb the bumps. Lower your saddle approximately 3–4cm/1–1½in to provide more space to manoeuvre. Concentrate on your line — not obstacles in your path.

High-speed, short downhills

On these downhills, you can usually see all the way to the bottom, and thus pick your line all the way to the lowest point. This is particularly useful since you can go as fast as the terrain permits for the entire downhill and maintain maximum momentum up the other side, which means a huge conservation of energy and a higher overall speed. Your first aim should be to select your line down the hill, and as far as possible up the other side, and then follow it through.

CONTROL ON DOWNHILLS DEMANDS SKILL AND A STRONG UPPER BODY.

Long downhills

Expect a combination of technical riding and relatively easy terrain on long downhills. Since you are unlikely to see the entire downhill from your starting point, you need to see it as something of a 'moving window'. Look ahead well in advance (about 15m/50ft, depending on your speed, or at least as far as the terrain allows you) and pick the line you intend following. Stick to this line and add to it in your mind's eye as you encounter new terrain. This may sound like a rather difficult task but it will, in essence, become second nature after riding for just a short while. You need to start the long downhill at a pace you are sure you can handle without too much difficulty. Do not be tempted to go too hard too soon, because exhaustion will set in and fatigue will result in mistakes — and a crash.

Technical downhills

These downhills should not be ridden at high speed without a proper inspection of the terrain beforehand, as you need to familiarize yourself with obstacles in order to navigate them safely. Even if you are familiar with the terrain but have not ridden it recently — especially after adverse weather conditions — you should still do a low-speed scout of the area to avoid any nasty surprises on your route.

Professional downhill racers usually walk their course beforehand, and practice each obstacle until they have found the best line and can do the course with confidence. It is a good idea to visualise the full length of the course in your mind's eye before attempting to race it — and remember all the hints and tips on technique you have read here. When tackling technical downhills, also be sure to wear additional protective gear, such as downhill helmets, full-finger gloves, body armour, and protective pants (such as the type used in motocross).

Switchback descents

Switchbacks consist of a series of short downhills without the uphill on the other side. As a result, you need to have your speed under control for the upcoming hairpin bend and any surprises it might offer. The most favourable technique is to map your line from bend to bend, but to factor in some distance at the end of each run for braking and setting up for the corner. Braking in the corner should be avoided at all costs, as this will impact quite severely on your ability to negotiate rough terrain, and the shift in your centre of gravity will fling you into the outside of the corner, making it much more difficult to negotiate the corner at speed.

BECAUSE YOU CAN SEE THE ENTIRE STRETCH OF A SHORT DOWNHILL BEFORE YOU TACKLE IT, YOU ARE ABLE TO PLAN YOUR ROUTE AND MAINTAIN YOUR MOMENTUM RIGHT UP THE OTHER SIDE.

A RELAXED BODY WILL HELP YOU MAINTAIN CONTROL ON A DOWNHILL.

DROPPING IN: STEP 1 SCOUT FOR A GOOD LOOKING LINE, AND APPROACH WITH A LITTLE SPEED (AN EASY ROLL WILL DO). AS THE FRONT WHEEL GOES OVER THE EDGE, MOVE YOUR WEIGHT RIGHT BACK OFF THE SADDLE AND ONLY USE THE REAR BRAKE (INITIALLY, ANYWAY – YOU CAN ALWAYS MAKE LIMITED USE OF THE FRONT BRAKE LATER).

DROPPING IN: STEP 2 ONCE YOU ARE ON A ROLL, EXTEND THE TRUNK OF YOUR BODY AND LEGS, KEEPING THEM SLIGHTLY BENT, AND GENTLY FEATHER THE REAR BRAKE (BE CAREFUL THAT YOUR BRAKE DOES NOT LOCK). KEEPING YOUR WEIGHT BACK WILL HELP INCREASE TRACTION. AS THE SLOPE LEVELS OFF, MOVE YOUR WEIGHT FORWARD OVER THE SADDLE.

Dropping in

Since descending an incline is as much a part of mountain biking as mud and climbs, it is important that you know when to ride an obstacle and when to choose not to. 'Dropping in' is one way of making your way down steep inclines. You simply shift your weight as far back as possible, and let the bike roll over the edge. Dropping in is best used on drops where there is enough of a slope that the front wheel can actually roll down it without getting stuck on a ditch or vertical obstruction on the way down. Do not use this technique on very steep, almost vertical drop-offs.

Dropping off

Dropping off is a technique that should be used on particularly steep, almost vertical drops that end on a level surface.

DROPPING OFF: STEP 1 AS YOU NEAR THE EDGE OF THE DROP-OFF, MOVE YOUR WEIGHT BACK AND PREPARE NOT ONLY TO PULL BACK ON THE HANDLEBARS BUT ALSO PEDAL FIRMLY WITH A SINGLE STROKE TO LIFT THE FRONT OF THE BIKE.

DROPPING OFF: STEP 2 YOU NEED TO APPROACH A DROP-OFF WITH REASONABLE SPEED. IF YOU HAVE TOO LITTLE SPEED, THE FRONT WHEEL WILL DROP INTO THE DIP, WHILE TOO MUCH SPEED WILL CARRY YOU OUT TOO FAR OVER THE EDGE AND YOU WILL LAND WITH A HARD IMPACT THAT WILL END EITHER IN A CRASH OR DAMAGE YOUR BIKE (MASTERING THE WHEELIE BEFOREHAND WILL BE INVALUABLE HERE).

The terrain

An understanding of the basic elements of different types of terrain will help you gain confidence — but only if you actually go out and ride them.

Big rocks and boulders

Large rocks are best avoided by riding around them wherever possible, or jumping them where the size and landing area behind the rock allows you to do this safely. At low speeds, and with larger rocks, you can use a special technique to ride up steep ledges and ridges. The sequence of events demands that you approach the ledge or rock at an easy pace (you can always increase the speed later when you get the hang of things) and in a reasonably powerful gear (about middle ring in the front, and about the middle of the cassette at the rear).

Small rocks and stones

This type of terrain presents a challenge to all riders, since they are rather like ball bearings and often cause you and the bike to slide. Both steering and braking become very difficult and you have to learn to take control under these conditions.

APPROACHING OBSTACLES: STEP 1 JUST BEFORE YOUR FRONT WHEEL ENCOUNTERS THE OBSTACLE, SIMULTANEOUSLY PULL UP ON THE HANDLEBARS AND APPLY POWER THROUGH THE DRIVE-TRAIN — RATHER LIKE DOING A WHEELIE. ONLY LIFT THE FRONT WHEEL HIGH ENOUGH SO THAT IT CAN MOUNT THE LOG OR LEDGE.

APPROACHING OBSTACLES: STEP 2 ONCE THE WHEEL IS SAFELY ON TOP OF THE LOG, MOVE YOUR WEIGHT FORWARD AS FAR AS POSSIBLE, SO THAT THE MOMENTUM IS MAINTAINED AND THE REAR WHEEL IS UNWEIGHTED (TEMPORARILY SHIFTING YOUR BODY TO REMOVE ALL WEIGHT).

APPROACHING OBSTACLES: STEP 3 BE SURE TO CONTINUE PEDALLING, AND THE REAR WHEEL WILL HIT THE OBSTACLE. BECAUSE MOST OF YOUR WEIGHT IS ON THE FRONT WHEEL AND YOU HAVE FORWARD MOMENTUM, THE REAR WHEEL WILL CLIMB UP THE LOG AND ROLL TO THE TOP. YOU CAN NOW MOVE YOUR WEIGHT BACK TO YOUR STANDARD RIDING POSITION.

A IF A RUT IS RELATIVELY NARROW AND NOT VERY DEEP, IT MAY BE EASIEST TO SIMPLY JUMP YOUR BIKE ACROSS.

B DEEP, WIDE RUTS MAY REQUIRE SKILFUL MANOEUVRING, BUT MUCH WILL ALSO DEPEND ON YOUR BODY POSITION.

Probably the most important fact to remember is that you cannot control your bike on stones and pebbles as well as you can on solid terrain. You thus need to learn to relax on the bike and go with the flow, to guide — rather than steer — the bike from one patch of solid ground to the next. The only way you can do this effectively is to choose a point on your line, aim for it — and go! It is almost not worth trying to steer at all, and the only way you can change direction is to shift your weight from side to side, to nudge the bike into a different direction.

Your braking habits also need to be revised. On downhill sections, you need to keep your weight back so that your rear wheel has better traction. Avoid using the front brake too much — especially on corners — and do not put more stress than necessary on the traction available on the front. Try to use the rear brake, and make only limited use of the front brake. Be sure that your brakes do not lock, as this will cause loose rocks and pebbles to roll under your wheels, and once this has happened you will gain rather than lose speed, with virtually all control over the bike lost.

Ruts

Always try to traverse ruts with your bike as horizontal as possible. Getting stuck in a rut will inevitably cause you to crash and probably damage your bike. Small ruts can be jumped (see page 43), but wider ruts may demand a different approach. If the rut is wide enough, you may simply be able to ride through it by shifting your weight back off the front wheel when it encounters the rut, pushing the wheel down into the rut, and then jerking it out again as it reaches the opposite side of the rut. Simply pedal through while shifting your weight forward. This technique is similar to that suggested for riding over big rocks or up ledges, except that, in this instance, you guide your front wheel through a trough instead of onto an obstacle.

The V-shaped rut caused by run-off water, however, is one of the most difficult to conquer. These ruts are usually about 50cm/20in wide and just as deep at the deepest part of the V. You may choose to simply carry your bike over, but there are various techniques that will get you over. Your best option is to wheelie the front wheel over the rut, and shift your weight slightly forward just before the rear wheel hits the rut — and keep on pedalling until you are out.

If you are stuck lengthwise in a rut, look for a spot where the sides are not too steep, and ride the bike out at that point. You could also use a sideways bunny hop (see page 42—43) to jump out, but if the rut is too deep, gently reduce speed, stop — and climb out.

Sand

Sand traps may be intimidating, but the technique is very similar to the one you would use to ride over loose rocks. Steering will be fruitless because the front wheel will only dig in and you will not be able to change the direction of your bike much. The correct action is as follows:

■ Approach the sandy part as fast as possible. Keep your weight back, and aim for the spot you want to reach.

■ Keep up speed by pedalling smoothly but powerfully. Riding through thick, loose sand is almost like surfing — simply go with the flow. A good tip to remember is that

tracks already made by other riders or motor cars are usually firmer because they have been compacted by the weight of the vehicle, and might be easier to ride.

Roots

Tree roots are the bane of many a rider and, when crossing the trail diagonally and at a slope, are guaranteed to cause a crash. Wet and slimy roots only make matters worse. Either carry your bike over or wheelie the front wheel over, and then move your weight forward to let the rear wheel roll over. Remember to keep the pressure off the drive-train or you will lose traction.

Logs

Logs should be treated much like big rocks and you should use the same technique to cross them. The only variation is that, by the time the rear wheel hits the log, the front wheel would have dropped off the other side. Be careful, therefore, not to move your weight too far forward during this stage. Small logs can be jumped using the bunny hop (see page 42—43).

LOGS MAKE CHALLENGING OBSTACLES, BUT START SMALL AND WORK YOUR WAY TO BIGGER OBSTACLES AS AND WHEN YOUR SKILL AND ABILITY IMPROVES.

WATER CROSSINGS CAN BE EXCITING — AND REFRESHING — BUT WATCH OUT
FOR SUBMERGED ROCKS, AND REMEMBER TO SERVICE THE BIKE MORE OFTEN
IF YOU ARE CROSSING WATER FREQUENTLY.

A GOOD CORNERING TECHNIQUE WILL HELP YOU TO CORNER FAST —
WITHOUT CRASHING.

Water crossings

Although the idea of crashing through a water course may be exhilarating, it is always a good idea to first check whether the water is not too deep and whether there are rocks or deep holes under the surface — even if you think you know the crossing well. When the crossing is unknown to you or you have not used it for a while, it is best to ride through slowly or, better still, climb off the bike and walk. In the words of Albert Iten, the famous Swiss downhill guru: 'It is better to carry your bike over the water, since water and mud will influence your shifting and braking, and is not good for your bike. Rather get your feet wet — they will dry out again.' If, however, you are confident that the crossing is safe, then feel free to blast through, but remember to keep your weight back.

Cornering

Even riders who have been riding for a long time often lack technique and lose speed when cornering on dirt roads and trails, and run the risk of crashing. Negotiating a corner can be divided into three phases: the entry, the actual corner and the exit. At the same time, you have to consider your speed, the terrain and your position on the bike.

Assessing the situation

Sometimes you carry your bike, but sometimes your bike carries you. Base your decision on what the situation or the terrain dictates.
■ Don't try new tricks far away from home, or in a place from which you may have to be rescued.
■ Don't attempt difficult manoeuvres when you are alone. Try to have friends with you — just in case you are injured, or to mentor you in mastering techniques and obstacles.
■ Don't try to tackle obstacles unless you are confident that you can, and have practised.
■ Most importantly, learn to do it properly!

1 2 3

■ **CORNERING: THE ENTRY OR APPROACH**
WHEN APPROACHING THE CORNER, TRY TO
READ THE TERRAIN. YOU SHOULD BE ABLE TO
JUDGE THE MAXIMUM SPEED YOU ARE ABLE TO
HANDLE, PICK THE BEST LINE AND JUDGE THE
SURFACE QUALITY, WHICH WILL INFLUENCE
YOUR TRACTION, AND HAVE SOME BEARING
ON THE PREVIOUS TWO ASPECTS TOO. ENTER
THE CORNER AT A SPEED YOU KNOW YOU CAN
MAINTAIN WHILE SMOOTHLY EXECUTING THE
CORNER. IN FACT, RATHER ENTER TOO SLOW
THAN TOO FAST. BRAKING IN A CORNER IS
ONE OF THE WORST THINGS YOU CAN DO.
STAY RELAXED ON THE BIKE AND MAKE FINAL
ADJUSTMENTS TO YOUR LINE AT THIS STAGE.

■ **CORNERING: THE CORNER** BY THIS STAGE,
YOU SHOULD HAVE YOUR LINE DEFINED, AND
YOU SHOULD BE AT THE CORRECT SPEED. AS
THE CORNER STARTS TO TURN, SHIFT YOUR
WEIGHT FORWARD AND OUTWARDS, TAKING
THE BIKE WITH YOU. TRY TO POSITION YOUR
WEIGHT OVER AN IMAGINARY POINT
SOMEWHERE BETWEEN THE FRONT HUB AND
THE CRANKS. WHEN LOOKING DOWN AT THIS
POINT, YOU SHOULD SEE THE OUTSIDE OF THE

FRONT WHEEL, WITH THE SIDE OF THE WHEEL
FACING THE OUTSIDE OF THE CORNER. YOU
CAN EVEN DROP A KNEE IN THE CORNER LIKE
A GRAND-PRIX MOTORCYCLIST. IF THE CORNER
IS NOT TOO SHARP AND YOU HAVE ENOUGH
GROUND CLEARANCE, YOU MAY EVEN TRY TO
SNEAK IN A FEW PEDAL STROKES IF THERE IS
ROOM FOR MORE SPEED. SOME RIDERS PREFER
TO KEEP THE OUTSIDE PEDAL DOWN AND PLACE
MORE WEIGHT ON IT, WITH LESS WEIGHT ON
THE SADDLE. THIS ALLOWS YOU TO BE MORE
RELAXED ON THE BIKE AND PROVIDES BETTER
GROUND CLEARANCE, BUT MAY INFLUENCE
YOUR BALANCE. PUSH DOWN ON THE SIDE
OF THE HANDLEBAR THAT IS ON THE INSIDE
OF THE CORNER TO PROVIDE EVEN MORE
TRACTION ON THE FRONT WHEEL. SERIOUS
DOWNHILL RACERS OFTEN KEEP THE PEDALS
LEVEL. THIS HELPS TO KEEP YOU BALANCED
AND READY TO SPRINT OUT OF THE CORNER.
IF YOU DO HAVE TO APPLY BRAKES, AVOID
USING THE FRONT BRAKE WHEREVER POSSIBLE
AS THE ADDED STRAIN ON THE FRONT MIGHT
COMPROMISE YOUR TRACTION, AND CAUSE
THE TYRE TO WASH OUT. THE REAR BRAKE

MAY SOMETIMES BE USED TO TEMPORARILY
PLACE THE BIKE IN A REAR-WHEEL SKID BY
LOCKING THE BRAKE FOR JUST A SPLIT
SECOND. BE WARNED, HOWEVER, THAT
YOU SHOULD NOT USE THIS TECHNIQUE ON
RECREATIONAL TRAILS SINCE IT MAY DAMAGE
THE TRAIL, WHICH IN TURN WILL CAUSE MORE
EROSION WHEN THE RAINS COME. SAVE IT FOR
RACE DAY, IN A CONTROLLED ENVIRONMENT.

■ **CORNERING: THE EXIT** THIS IS YOUR
OPPORTUNITY TO MAKE UP SPEED IF YOU TOOK
THE CORNER TOO SLOW, OR TO GAIN EVEN
MORE SPEED IF YOU TOOK THE CORNER AT
OPTIMUM SPEED. AS YOU NEAR THE END OF
THE BEND AND YOU START TO STRAIGHTEN
YOUR BODY, YOU CAN BEGIN TO APPLY
CONSIDERABLY MORE POWER TO THE PEDALS.
YOU WILL THEN BE CATAPULTED FORWARD AS
YOU ACCELERATE OUT OF THE CORNER.
SPRINTING OUT OF THE CORNER WILL GIVE
YOU THE EDGE OVER OTHER RIDERS, AND WILL
CATAPULT YOU INTO THE STRAIGHT AT HIGH
SPEED. SOMETIMES, HOWEVER, IT IS WISE TO
WALK IT INSTEAD, AND BE ABLE TO ENJOY THE
REST OF THE RIDE.

Getting Fit and Keeping Fit

it is important to know that cycling is a multifaceted sport. It is a discipline that requires insight and appreciation of the sciences, especially sport-specific training principles and, more specifically, the principles surrounding the theories of endurance. Furthermore, cycling is a dynamic activity that may be categorised into various disciplines — time trials, road cycling, downhill racing, cross country and so on. Components such as nutrition and supplementation, heart-rate training and, most importantly, determining and setting goals, all play a key role in the success of the rider. A closer look at these areas will help both the novice and advanced mountain biker in the preparation and enjoyment of their pastime.

Road cycling has been at the forefront of cycling for many years, but only in the past 10 to 15 years have we seen mountain biking emerge as a unique cycling activity. Many professional road cyclists have ventured into mountain biking, bringing with them the associated scientific training. Today, the most experienced mountain bikers are professional athletes who take pride in both their training and their preparation. This, of course, has had considerable influence on the mountain-biking community at large, with the novice or intermediate mountain biker intent on doing everything correctly right from the outset. We live in a highly technological age where ergogenic aids, like heart-rate monitors and legal performance-enhancing products, are to be expected. This chapter exposes the basic formula to success in the sport of mountain biking, whether you are a novice or advanced cyclist.

Fun and GAMES

The games we play and plan when mountain biking could look as follows:

G **Goal** setting sets the process in motion.

A Goal setting allows for an **action** plan to be determined, which in turn promotes the appropriate attitude you require for personal success.

M An action plan will provide you with the important **motivation** to stay consistent throughout the challenge. If you are motivated, you will 'see' yourself achieve success by using mental rehearsal or mental imagery. Remember, positive thinking invites success — but don't forget that it is accompanied by lots of hard work!

E It is absolutely vital that you **enjoy** the challenge. Fun and enjoyment make the entire trip worthwhile.

S If you are able to adhere to and achieve all of the above, you will be able to record many a **success** story in your training logbook and swap plenty of impressive stories about your prowess with other off-roaders around the post-race campfire.

above and opposite CYCLING REGULARLY WITH OTHER MOUNTAIN BIKERS AND BEING ACCOUNTABLE TO THEM HELPS YOU KEEP EXERCISING, WHILE ALSO HELPING YOU ACHIEVE THE GOALS YOU HAVE SET.

MAKE SURE THAT THE GOALS YOU SET FOR YOURSELF ARE REALISTIC. IF THEY ARE UNATTAINABLE, YOU WILL INEVITABLY BECOME DEMOTIVATED.

Goal setting

Goal orientation or the setting of sporting goals is the most important step for an athlete or mountain biker. This sets the precedent or course that should be followed by the cyclist to achieve success relative to his or her aspirations. No matter what level you are at, it is vital to decide what you would like to achieve.

Goal setting is personal and should be treated as a contract or agreement with yourself. By standing accountable for your own actions and efforts, success and fun are just around the next corner. The setting of goals allows the cyclist to plot his or her personal route. The goals determine the journey and it is up to the rider to get what he or she can out of the 'ride'. Setting goals allows the cyclist to adopt a recipe for success, but it is important to understand the criteria:

■ **Personal goals** Goals need to be personal. If you particularly enjoy downhill racing but set yourself the goal of completing a major cross-country race simply because everyone else is, you will set yourself up for disappointment and/or failure.

■ **Progressive** Goals should be both systematic and progressive. The easy way to ensure that you achieve this is to set short-term (six months), intermediate (up to 12 months) and long-term (ultimate) goals.

■ **Attainable** It is pointless to set goals that are not achievable. Remember that success breeds success.

■ **Realistic** This criterion is closely related to the attainability of your goals, and you will be doomed to fail if those goals are unrealistic. Goals that are too easy or too difficult lay the foundation for frustration.

■ **Adjustable** If you are injured, ill or have achieved goals too easily, they may need to be reformulated.

■ **Flexibility** You may find an opportunity to achieve success in an event that was not part of your original plan. Be sure to assess a situation and decide whether, in the grander scheme of things, it may be worth your while to tackle an event that will promote your over-all 'goal plan' in the long run.

■ **Enjoyable** The process needs to be enjoyable. You will stay motivated if you enjoy what you are striving to achieve and the path you have chosen to get you there.

The art of training

Success often comes just by chance. However, consistent 'winning' is not a matter of chance — but rather a result of careful planning and training.

Unlike road cycling, where there is not much else to do except concentrate on your cadence — and try to stay alive — mountain biking offers three distractions: the scenery, the company and the difficulties or joys of the terrain. Mountain bikers, therefore, can't help emphasising the 'outing', and can be forgiven for neglecting the formalized component of training.

However, endurance training is a science and should be treated as such. No matter what level you are, you should approach the sport with at least some scientific appreciation. To complete an event or to achieve line honours will certainly require some scientific training.

Basic training principles

■ **Bike set-up** Ensure that your bike has been set up correctly for you and the specific event in which you are participating (downhill as opposed to cross-country, for example). The incorrect bike set-up or technique could lead to the novice or even the highly talented cyclist wasting valuable energy.

■ **The overload principle** Apply the progressive overload principle. Increase overload — intensity or duration — by 10 per cent a week. For example, if you are a novice starting from scratch, ride three times per week (for about 30 minutes) at a low intensity (about 60 per cent), increasing the ride duration by 10 per cent every week (see also heart-rate training on page 60).

■ **Specific training** To improve your fitness for mountain biking you need to ride your mountain bike, and it won't help that much if, for example, you run in order to become fit for mountain biking. Many mountain bikers supplement their training with other activities, but these are only incorporated in their training regime after specific training has been scheduled. Therefore, to improve as a mountain biker, off-road riding is essential. Road cycling may, however, complement mountain-bike fitness, giving you a break from the demands that riding off the road entails. If you are a novice and only have the opportunity to train three times a week, spend that time on your mountain bike.

■ **Develop (aerobic) foundation** Training is rather like building a house. You first need to build a foundation before the rest of the house can be completed and can stand firm. The foundation phase exposes the body to

THE SUCCESS OF YOUR TRAINING PROGRAMME DEMANDS THAT YOU DO REGULAR BICYCLE-SPECIFIC EXERCISES, SUCH AS STRETCHING THE MUSCLES IN YOUR LEGS AND UPPER BODY. IDEALLY, THESE EXERCISES MAY BE DONE WITH YOUR BICYCLE AS FACILITATOR.

One step at a time

■ **Base development phase**
(3 weeks–3 months)

The novice rider can take three or more weeks of low-intensity riding (up to 70 per cent of the maximum heart rate) to develop the foundation of the season.

■ **Strength phase**
(2 weeks–2 months)

During this phase, the rider develops strength. Complementary strength-training sessions — such as free weights and gym equipment — may also be done, while specific strength development can be done on the bike itself. The cyclist may ride very hilly terrain or even isolate each limb while riding (pedalling with one leg at a time only). The aim in this phase is to strengthen the body, and this is the first step in achieving the ability to 'power' down hills or to be able to 'power' up and over hills during an event. Power is the combination of strength and speed.

■ **Overload or specific phase**
(2 weeks–2 months)

This phase requires plenty of discipline because it is easy for simple sessions to develop into moderate ones because the cyclist is riding too hard. Remember, 'more' and/or 'harder' are not always better. If you are on an 'easy' programme, keep it that way and save that effort for the Big One. This phase is probably the most enduring but most exciting phase, because riders have progressively overloaded their bodies and are now equipped to engage in some dynamic training sessions and races that will prepare them for the big race. Although you should continue to develop strength during this phase of your training, reduce it to about 15 per cent of total training. The challenging and dynamic qualities for a mountain biker to attain are: speed endurance (the ability to cycle fast for long periods) and power (combining speed and strength in an event where you have to close a gap or attack). These make racing a very exciting prospect indeed!

■ **Taper and peak phase**
(2 weeks–4 weeks)

This period in your training is often the most frustrating phase because you have to cut back by 10 per cent a week leading up to the major race of the season. You may find yourself going into withdrawal, and often feel that you are losing the fitness you worked so hard to build up. But rest assured that you will find yourself peaking on race day if you taper correctly. During the taper phase, training continues but you are now in a much better state to complete quality sessions. In those races you cycled in preparation for the big event, you will record good results.

■ **Restoration phase**
(2 weeks–1 or 2 months

This phase is important as it is now that you will allow your body to recover from the race, or the season, and cut back on training. Take a holiday, returning refreshed and ready for the next season.

easy training, allowing it to prepare for more gruelling or higher intensity sessions. It is this phase that equips the cyclist's body for continual overload for a long period. If a mountain biker has a limited (aerobic) base or foundation, they are limited to a short season. The more extensive the base, the longer the cyclist can race with consistency.

■ **Predetermined training phases** Identify the season's events that are most important to you. The body can peak approximately three to four times a year. Thereafter, minor or sub-peaks are achievable. The phases below will then be planned around important races or events.

■ **Rest** Rest is a right, and not a privilege. Once you have identified the races you intend to cycle, the next step is to plan the rest days or periods that facilitate the specific phases of training. The body works in cycles of 21 to 26 days, and after that period planned rest — over and above your weekly rest — is required. By predetermining these rest cycles, you will be able to ensure controlled overload. At times, it may be difficult to assess or analyse the overload on your own body. The body goes through intense overload — known as 'super compensation' — during the overload or specific phase. If you continue to overload your body without planned rest, you will 'over-train' your body and burn out.

■ **Weekly and monthly training cycles:** As mentioned earlier, 21- to 26-day cycles, or seven-day cycles, may facilitate the planning of training.

Following the cycles

Monthly cycles

■ Week one (seven days)	Introduction overload/maintenance
■ Week two	Overload
■ Week three	Rest or recovery

Weekly cycles

Training week

■ Day one	Rest or active rest (up to 65–70 per cent of maximum heart rate)
■ Day two	Easy ride (up to 70 per cent)
■ Day three	Increased intensity or duration
■ Day four	Easy ride (up to 75 per cent)
■ Day five	Moderate (up to 80 per cent) session or time trial
■ Day six	Easy ride or rest
■ Day seven	Moderate ride or long, slow distance ride

Recovery week

■ Day one	30–60 minutes, and a moderate- to hard-tempo session (up to 85 per cent)
■ Day two	60 minutes, and easy (up to 75 per cent)
■ Day three	Rest or active rest
■ Day four	Rest
■ Day five	30–90 minutes, and easy (up to 70 per cent)
■ Day six	30–60 minutes, and easy (up to 70 per cent)
■ Day seven	Race, or race-assimilation session

Heart-rate monitors

Heart-rate monitors have revolutionized training and racing, but you need to understand how monitors work.

Negatives

Many problems lie simply in human error, the lack of education and the mountain biker's inadequate training.

■ **What do you want?** You need to identify what you want from a heart-rate monitor. There are many models and, although all give feedback on the heart rate, the biofeedback is different for each monitor. In other words, you may have a monitor that provides too much or too little of what you require.

■ **Read the manual!** About 80 per cent of all pur-chasers of advanced equipment do not read the instructions.

■ **Know your training zones or parameters** Without knowing the correct training intensities or percent-ages, you will over- or under-train, so be sure to ascertain your maximum and resting heart rates. Unfortunately, your theoretical maximum heart rate is insufficient because this is the standard used by runners rather than cyclists. Competitive riders should test their maximum heart rate every two months, as it changes with training. Your resting heart rate should be recorded every day as this allows you to use the Karvonen Equation:

Max HR — Rest HR x % + Rest HR

Your training heart rate is thus maximum heart rate minus resting heart rate, multiplied by the intensity at which you would like to train, plus resting heart rate.

■ **Consistent use** Use the monitor consistently, as this promotes scientific training.

■ **When to use it** Use the biofeedback as an analysing exercise, and not as a dictator in a race. If you are part of a breakaway at the start, the monitor is there to *guide* your effort — you might be at maximum effort, but when the nature of the race changes, your heart rate drops.

THE HEART-RATE MONITOR HAS REVOLUTIONIZED THE CYCLIST'S TRAINING PROGRAMME, AND HAS PROGRESSED AND TRANSFORMED INTO EQUIPMENT THAT IS BOTH USER FRIENDLY AND FASHIONABLE. BUT THIS ERGOGENIC AID IS USELESS IF THE RIDER DOES NOT UNDERSTAND ITS USES OR APPRECIATE THE TECHNOLOGY AND OPERATING PROCEDURES VITAL TO ITS SUCCESS AS A FACILITATOR. A HEART-RATE MONITOR IS FAR MORE THAN A SIMPLE STOP WATCH! IF YOU ARE UNSURE OF HOW TO USE IT, CONSULT A PROFESSIONAL.

■ **Accuracy** The monitor does away with guesswork for training and racing, and provides defined parameters.

■ **Scientific training** The monitor places scientific training methods within the reach of all riders.

■ **Variations in training** Instead of using time, the monitor uses your heart rate to determine rest and intervals, allowing for variation and holding your interest in training.

■ **Feedback** The heart-rate monitor provides day-to-day feedback on the condition of the cyclist.

The heart-rate monitor can thus optimize training, but do not discard your own intuition in favour of technology because racing depends, too, on personal experience. The monitor should only be a *guide*.

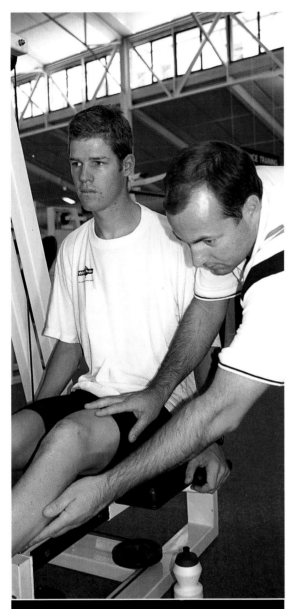

YOUR FITNESS LEVEL MAY ALSO DEPEND ON YOUR TRAINER'S SKILLS.

Positives

■ **Monitoring intensity** Monitors optimize training. Determine parameters (see page 57) so 'easy days' remain easy, and 'difficult days' remain challenging.

■ **Your personal coach** The heart-rate monitor can simplify your programme and can act as your 'coach'. Training effectively allows for the concise recording and determination of what works for you.

Helpful hints

■ Once a week, go out with friends and 'play' on your bike — this will not only improve your cycling skills, but you will also learn from each other. Some BMX clubs have a mountain-bike category at their BMX events. Practise jumping, landing, cornering, hopping and balancing. Don't underestimate the power of 'play' as part of your training schedule. If you have time and money, motocross is also an excellent alternative for enhancing off-road bicycle-handling skills. For cross country, fitness is a must; for downhilling and the duel, power, fitness *and* advanced handling skills are essential.

■ Why do so many excercise bikes, pieces of home-gym equipment and bicycles moulder away in basements, garages or lofts? Because, for exercise to really work, you need the social interaction. If you are accountable to a riding buddy, you will ride consistently, and go from strength to strength. It is also a very good idea to join your local mountain-bike club to find out about routes and meet fellow enthusiasts.

■ If you have enough time to train some weeks, but others are too busy with business trips or overtime, simply try to be consistent: spend less time in the saddle, but try to do something every day (cycle commuting is really helpful here). Cycling is a life style.

Supplementary training

Research has shown that weight training at a gym can further enhance the performance of a mountain biker. The first goal of supplementary training is that it must complement the off-road training. Resistance or weight training must, therefore, be specific to the needs and goals of the individual rider and the event or race so that it does not adversely affect training sessions aimed specifically at bike riding. See page 57.

Spinning

Spinning — pedalling at more than 100 revolutions per minute (rpm) — originated in the USA, but was formalized as a group exercise in South Africa. It is done as an aerobic class on stationary bikes, and may

SPINNING ALLOWS YOU TO FOCUS ON PARTICULAR AREAS OF YOUR BODY WITHOUT THE DISTRACTIONS OF AN OFF-ROAD RIDE.

complement the training you do on your mountain bike. Spinning is done indoors, ensuring greater consistency in training, and overloads the anaerobic system, promoting both leg speed and power. Aerobic training is limited unless the rider is disciplined to ride at lower intensities.

Home-conditioning

Strength training is successful only if you overload all the muscle fibres. This can be done with resistance training. The advanced mountain biker should incorporate a gym session two to three times a week in the 'strengthening phase', and once or twice a week during the specific phase. During the taper and peak phase, only a weekly session is required — and no gym at all in the two weeks preceding the race.

LATISSIMUS DORSI

TRICEPS

PECTORAL MUSCLE

BICEP

ABDOMINAL MUSCLES

OBLIQUE MUSCLES

FOREARMS

LOWER LUMBAR

GLUTEUS MAXIMUS

QUADRICEPS MUSCLES

HAMSTRING MUSCLE

GASTROCNEMIUS MUSCLES

SOLEUS

ACHILLES TENDON

TIBIALIS ANTERIOR

THE MUSCLES OF THE UPPER BODY SHOULD ALSO BE CONDITIONED BY YOUR HOME FITNESS PROGRAMME.

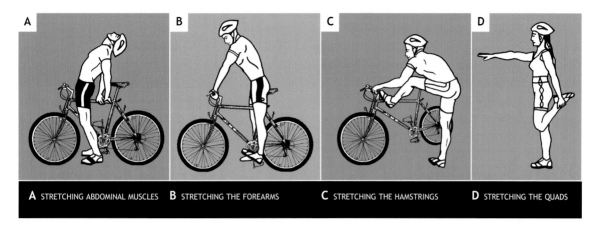

A STRETCHING ABDOMINAL MUSCLES   **B** STRETCHING THE FOREARMS   **C** STRETCHING THE HAMSTRINGS   **D** STRETCHING THE QUADS

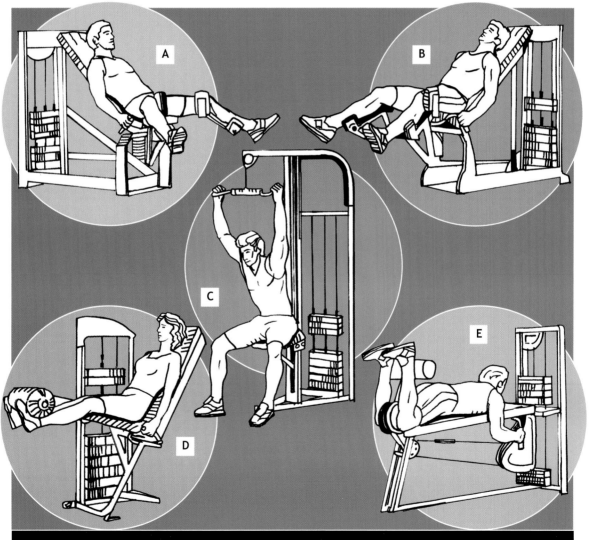

THE LEG ABDUCTOR MACHINE WILL WORK BOTH THE INNER THIGH (A) AND THE OUTER THIGH (B), WHILE PULLING WEIGHTS (C) WILL HELP DEVELOP THE BICEPS AND THE TRICEPS. THE LEG EXTENSION MACHINE (D) WILL WORK THE QUADS, AND THE LEG-CURL MACHINE (E) WILL DEVELOP THE HAMSTRING.

Strength programme for advanced riders

Understanding your own capabilities will equip you with the basic knowledge to plan your own workouts — whether you are a novice or an advanced rider. Every rider has specific strengths and weaknesses, so training in the same way as other riders does not necessarily mean that you will perform like them. Set your own goals and targets and do quality training sessions that are specifically geared for your own racing season.

For the advanced rider, two to three sets of 8–12 repetitions should be carried out at 85 per cent of maximum repetition (maximum repetition = maximum effort in one attempt).

Stretching

As the rider ages (25 and over), muscles lose elasticity but with regular stretching, deterioration is limited and the risk of injury is reduced. The lower back (lumbar), posterior (gluteus) and hamstring are areas of concern because cycling requires a 30-degree flexion of the knee. If the rider does not stretch regularly, the muscles become inflexible. Hold the stretch for 10–20 seconds. For flexibility, complete a 45- to 60-minute stretching session once a week, holding the stretch for up to 60 seconds. The stretch and body position are passive and the stretch is progressive. When working on flexibility, increase the stretch every 20 seconds.

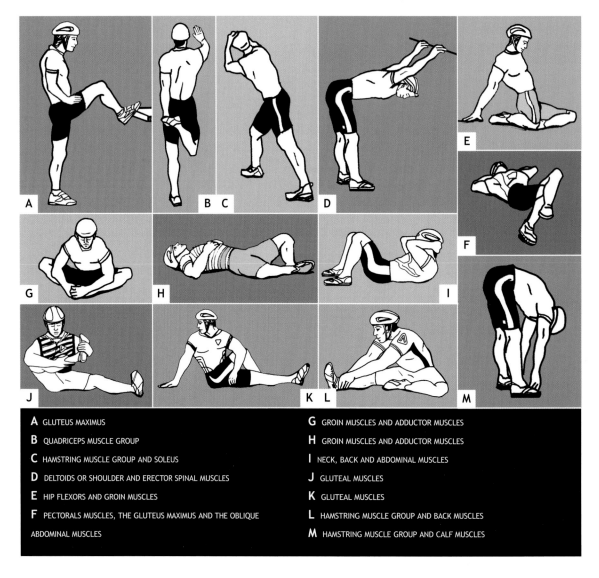

A GLUTEUS MAXIMUS

B QUADRICEPS MUSCLE GROUP

C HAMSTRING MUSCLE GROUP AND SOLEUS

D DELTOIDS OR SHOULDER AND ERECTOR SPINAL MUSCLES

E HIP FLEXORS AND GROIN MUSCLES

F PECTORALS MUSCLES, THE GLUTEUS MAXIMUS AND THE OBLIQUE
ABDOMINAL MUSCLES

G GROIN MUSCLES AND ADDUCTOR MUSCLES

H GROIN MUSCLES AND ADDUCTOR MUSCLES

I NECK, BACK AND ABDOMINAL MUSCLES

J GLUTEAL MUSCLES

K GLUTEAL MUSCLES

L HAMSTRING MUSCLE GROUP AND BACK MUSCLES

M HAMSTRING MUSCLE GROUP AND CALF MUSCLES

To cycle, you require 'pure' and regular energy — especially over long-distances. Endurance riders need to metabolise fat as an energy source, so food and liquid should be 'pure' energy sources.

Try to take in unrefined — as opposed to refined — products: rye bread rather than white bread, baked potato rather than fries. Many products have preservatives and colourants that influence the 'pure' source of energy.

Eat foodstuffs that originate from the ground. Fruit and vegetables have high levels of antioxidants, which include vitamin C, vitamin E, Beta-Carotene, vitamin B6 and 12 and selenium. Antioxidants help detoxify the body. Exercise and the digestive process produce free radicals, which impede the functioning of the body, so it is important to supplement with antioxidants.

Water

About 75 per cent of the body consists of water, facilitating detoxification. As carbohydrates

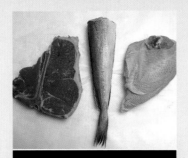
PROTEIN: RED MEAT, FISH AND CHICKEN.

are broken down to glycogen, they are stored as one molecule of glycogen to three molecules of water. The mountain biker should, therefore, drink as much water as possible (about eight to 14 glasses a day) and avoid fizzy, caffeinated drinks that limit the absorption of certain nutrients.

Protein

We need protein to ensure that the 23 amino acids we require are supplemented. Amino acids are the building blocks that facilitate rebuilding and repair after exercise. Meat, chicken, fish, beans, grains and legumes contain amino acids, particularly the six essential amino acids the body cannot produce itself.

Fat

Recent studies have shown that if the body takes in plant and vegetable fat on a regular basis, it is equipped to utilise more fat as an energy source. (Animal fat has a high cholesterol content

and is not a good energy source). Many people are thus turning to the 60–30–30 diet, where 60 per cent is carbohydrate, 30 per cent protein and 30 per cent fat.

Food on the go

In an event, you need a drink that combines electrolytes and carbohydrates. Read the package of products to check whether they provide the energy you will require, but bananas and fruit cake are favourite cyclists' fuel.

Post-race energy replacement allows your body to replenish creatine and glycogen. Rehydrate and replace electrolytes and glycogen. After 45 minutes, take in protein to replenish amino acids and creatine. Antioxidants are needed, too.

Many products may claim to promote performance, but it is important to follow sound nutritional advice rather than rely on the word of manufacturers. Take a multivitamin and multimineral, but be sure to consult your sports physician or dietician first.

DRINK 8 TO 14 GLASSES OF WATER A DAY.

PLANT AND VEGETABLE FATS.

Maintaining your Mountain Bike

a mountain bike is a complex, yet simple and efficient machine, and its components are designed to accommodate stress. It is, however, almost certain that your bicycle *will* break down at some point, and this may be prevented — or the damage easily repaired — if you have the correct tools and some basic knowledge.

Cleaning materials

To keep your bike clean and avoid unnecessary wear on its parts, you will need the following materials:
■ Bucket of clean water
■ Bucket of hot, soapy water (use household cleaner such as washing powder or dishwashing liquid)
■ Degreaser (either environment-friendly citrus-based solvent, or paraffin or kerosene)
■ Assortment of brushes (a long, thin brush to get into tight spots, a large one with soft bristles for the frame, and a hard one for the rims, and tyres; a toothbrush provides good access to nooks and crannies)
■ Soft, dry cloth (to polish and dry the bike)
■ Automatic chain cleaner (optional — they usually work quite well and are more convenient)

Cleaning methods

■ Place the bike in a workstand or do it European style and hang the bike from a sling.
■ Rinse the bike with a bucket of clean water or a low-pressure hose to rid it of most of the grime and dirt. Keep the spray away from the bearings to prevent water from being forced past the seals.
■ Remove the wheels and wash them separately.
■ Use the degreaser to dissolve the old grease and oil on the sprockets, chain rings, chain and rear derailleur pulley wheels.
■ Using the warm, soapy water, wash the bike from the top down, starting at the saddle and handlebars, and finishing at the cranks and chain rings.

■ Scrub the brake blocks and inspect them for excessive wear and foreign objects that may be embedded in the rubber.
■ Inspect the cables and cable housings for damage or wear. They should be replaced if damaged or worn.
■ Wash the wheels and inspect the sidewall of the rim and spoke holes for damage or any sign of cracking. Also inspect the tyres for damage, paying particular attention to the sidewalls.
■ Check the wheel bearings for wear by holding the wheel in one hand and turning the axle with the other. The axle should turn smoothly (although the grease will result in a slight drag). If there is noticeable play or roughness, you need to service the hubs. The same applies to the cranks.
■ With the bike in the stand, turn the cranks and try to rock them from side to side. They should turn smoothly, with no lateral play at all. Make a mental list of any damage or potential problems, and be sure to tackle these later.

above A WORKSTAND OR SLING WILL ALLOW EASIER MAINTENANCE.
opposite FOR PEACE OF MIND, CARRY A REPAIR KIT WITH YOU.

Keep it lubed!

Most parts of your mountain bike need to be kept clean and well lubricated so that they operate smoothly and reliably, and remain in good working order.

The chain

Do not be tempted to use normal household or engine oil on your bicycle chain. Rather use a bicycle-specific chain lubricant, which has been specially formulated for the conditions in which you will ride your bike. Dry-condition chain lubricant will not attract dust and will wash off in water. Wet-condition lubricant is water resistant, but will attract dust. Normal oil, on the other hand, is not only messy, but will attract both dust and sand, forming an abrasive paste that will devour your drive-train.

The seat post

When washing and cleaning the bike, coat the seat post with a thin layer of grease to prevent it from getting stuck inside the frame.

Suspension forks

Most modern suspension forks tend to use the damping fluid as a lubricant and need not be lubricated. If the forks need external lubrication, use the lubricant supplied by the manufacturer, or lithium-free grease. Using a simple, standard lubricant could cause degradation of the bushes — the sliding surfaces in a telescopic type suspension fork — and eventually, failure of the shocks.

Hubs

When you spin the wheel and the hubs feel rough, they will need to be disassembled to be serviced (special tools, such as two cone spanners, are required). If pitted, the cones for the bearings — and the bearings themselves — will have to be replaced. The tracks along which the bearings run must be greased. Some quality after-market hubs — bought for the purposes of upgrading your standard equipment — are equipped with sealed cartridge hubs and, if this is the case, the cartridge bearing may be replaced as a complete unit.

CHAIN
LUBRICANT: DRY-CONDITION OR
WET-CONDITION BICYCLE-SPECIFIC
CHAIN LUBRICANT

SEAT POST
LUBRICANT: GREASE

FRONT SUSPENSION
LUBRICANT: LITHIUM-FREE GREASE
OR THE LUBRICANT SUPPLIED
BY THE MANUFACTURER

HUBS
LUBRICANT: GREASE

CERTAIN COMPONENTS OF YOUR MOUNTAIN BIKE DEMAND SPECIFIC LUBRICANTS, RATHER THAN SIMPLE HOUSEHOLD LUBRICANTS.

Essential tools

Bicycle-specific tools

These tools are specifically used to maintain bicycles and most of these can be obtained from a bicycle shop.

Essentials

Be practical about what to take, but the list of spares and tools below is the minimum you should carry with you.

Generic tools

Apart from bicycle-specific and other essential tools, you may well need the following generic tools in an emergency:

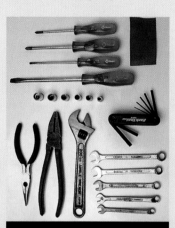

WITHOUT THESE BICYCLE-SPECIFIC TOOLS, YOU WILL NOT BE ABLE TO SERVICE YOUR BIKE PROPERLY.

- PAIR OF CABLE CUTTERS
- CHAIN-RIVETING TOOL
- CHAIN WHIP
- CRANK PULLER
- SET OF FLAT CONE WRENCHES
- FREE-WHEEL SPLINED SOCKET
- SET OF HEADSET WRENCHES TO MATCH YOUR BICYCLE HEADSET (IF YOUR BIKE DOES NOT HAVE AN AHEADSET™ SYSTEM)
- GOOD FOOT OR HAND PUMP (IF YOU ARE ABLE TO AFFORD IT, YOU MAY ALSO DECIDE TO INVEST IN A QUALITY FLOOR- OR TRACK-PUMP)
- SPOKE WRENCH (IT IS IMPORTANT THAT IT CATERS FOR A VARIETY OF DIFFERENT SIZES)
- SET OF TYRE LEVERS

LEAVING HOME WITHOUT THESE TOOLS MAY MEAN A LONG WALK IF YOU HAVE A BREAKDOWN EN ROUTE.

- AT LEAST ONE SPARE TUBE WITH THE CORRECT VALVE TYPE SPECIFIC TO YOUR RIM AND PUMP
- A STANDARD BICYCLE PUNCTURE-REPAIR KIT WITH A VARIETY OF PATCHES OF DIFFERENT SHAPES AND SIZES
- BICYCLE-SPECIFIC MULTI-TOOL (WHICH SHOULD INCLUDE ALL-IN-ONE ALLEN KEYS, SCREWDRIVER, ETC. AND OTHER FEATURES SUITED TO EMERGENCY BICYCLE REPAIRS)
- CHAIN-RIVETING TOOL
- SET OF TYRE LEVERS
- GOOD HAND OR FOOT PUMP
- SMALL POCKET KNIFE
- LEATHERMAN-TYPE TOOL (OPTIONAL)
- FLAT PIECE OF RUBBER (OR PIECE OF TYRE LINER) TO REPAIR TYRE CUTS

THESE ESSENTIAL TOOLS CAN BE BOUGHT FROM A HARDWARE STORE.

- SET OF PHILIPS AND FLAT-TIPPED SCREWDRIVERS
- SET OF METRIC OPEN-END AND RING-COMBINATION WRENCHES (6MM–17MM SHOULD BE FINE)
- SET OF SOCKETS (6MM–17MM)
- SET OF METRIC ALLEN KEYS
- SMALL ADJUSTABLE WRENCH
- GOOD PAIR OF UTILITY PLIERS
- PAIR OF LONG-NOSE PLIERS

A handy toolbox

- Spare brake-cable inner
- Spare gear-cable inner
- 1m/3ft brake cable
- 1m/3ft gear-cable outer-casing
- Spare chain
- Two pairs rubber brake blocks
- Spare rear derailleur
- Bottle of chain lubricant

Basic adjustments

Knowing how to do basic maintenance will allow you to enjoy some independence almost immediately.

Adjusting the tension of the brake cable

Method Each brake lever has a cable 'barrel' adjuster, which has a 'hollow' bolt with a lengthwise slot and a lock nut that screws onto the hollow bolt. This bolt screws into the brake lever, and can be screwed in or out. The other end allows the cable casing to fit into it, while the cable outer passes through the length of the bolt or barrel adjuster.

    Adjust By unscrewing the barrel adjuster, you will lengthen the cable casing, increasing the tension of the cable inner and moving the pads closer to the rim (or disc rotor).

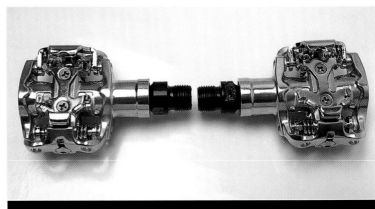

LEFT- AND RIGHT-HAND PEDALS HAVE OPPOSITE THREADS.

Adjusting the gear cables

Method The same principle applies as in adjusting the break cable. There is usually a barrel adjuster on the gear shifter and the derailleur ends of the cable. Leave the front barrel adjuster three turns unscrewed and make the adjustments at the rear derailleur. Your derailleur is equipped with two 'limiting screws' to restrict the movement of the derailleur.

    Adjust Increasing the tension in the cable shifts the derailleur up and thus moves the chain onto the next biggest sprocket. By decreasing the tension, you shift down to the smaller sprocket. Make sure you have downshifted all the way and the chain is on the smallest sprocket. With the chain on the middle ring in the front, shift the right-hand shifter one 'click'. If it does not make it onto the bigger sprocket, increase the cable tension by unscrewing the barrel adjuster. If the shift moved the chain too much, then slacken the tension in the cable by screwing in (in a clockwise direction) the barrel adjuster until the required movement has been achieved.

REAR DERAILLEUR WITH A BARREL ADJUSTER AT BOTTOM RIGHT. SCREWING THE ADJUSTER IN SLACKENS THE TENSION.

THE BOLT THAT HOLDS THE SEAT-POST IN THE FRAME IS TIGHTENED WITH A QUICK-RELEASE LEVER OR COLLAR CLAMP.

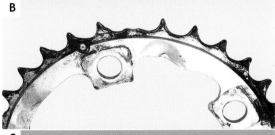

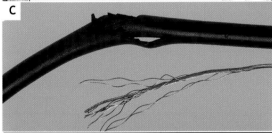

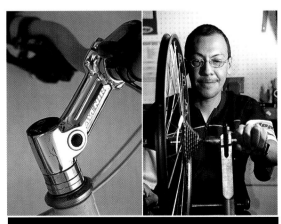

A TAKE SPECIAL CARE OF THE TYRE'S SIDEWALLS, THE WEAK SPOT WHERE FAILURE IS MOST LIKELY TO OCCUR.

B REPLACE A WORN CHAIN AND RING AS OFTEN AS NECESSARY.

C NEGLECTED CABLES CAN SERIOUSLY IMPAIR THE BIKE'S ABILITY TO SHIFT AND BRAKE WITH EFFICIENCY.

Preventative maintenance

Prevention is better — and cheaper — than cure.

The wheels

The wheels take the most abuse, so inspect the tyres for cuts, protruding objects and abrasions, paying attention to the sidewalls. Replace or repair the tyres immediately if in doubt. Roughness of, or play in the wheel bearings, should also be addressed.

Check the wheels for loose spokes, rim trueness (a perfect circle and flat disc) and the integrity of the rim itself (minute hairline cracks are telltale signs of impending rim failure). If you do not feel comfortable doing these adjustments, most specialist bike shops will do it for you.

The chain

Replace the chain every six months if you ride regularly and every three months if you participate in races often or it will wear down the gears and sprockets, which are somewhat more costly to replace.

The cables

Check the gear and brake cables for signs of wear (fraying, corrosion, or outer-casing failure), and replace them immediately if necessary. Cables are relatively cheap in comparison to other vital components, but they can be the cause of many serious problems if they are ignored. Never lubricate the cables. Rather replace both the cables and casing if they are corroded.

The handlebars

Check your handlebars for bends and cracks especially the clamp area of the stem. Loose handlebar grips should be glued back on or replaced with new ones. Loose bar-ends must also be adjusted and tightened.

The bottom bracket

When cleaning your bike, check the crank bearings, or bottom bracket, for play and have them replaced if this is the case. The bottom bracket on all modern mountain bikes is a sealed unit and cannot, therefore, be serviced. It needs to be replaced when worn.

THE AREA WHERE THE STEM CLAMPS TO THE HANDLEBAR NEEDS PARTICULAR ATTENTION.

TAKE CARE OF YOUR WHEELS, AMONG THE MOST IMPORTANT COMPONENTS OF YOUR BIKE.

The frame

When washing your bike, examine the frame for rust or cracking, paying special attention to the weld and headset areas.

The headset

Check the status of the headset bearings by activating the bike's front brakes. Rock the bike forwards and backwards. There should be no clicking noise or movement from the headset bearings. If there is, adjust or replace them immediately. Failure to do so can result in a loss of control because you will not be able to steer properly.

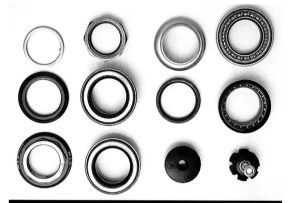

TYPICAL COMPONENTS OF THE HEADSET ASSEMBLY.

Problem	Reason	Solution
Gears jumping or not shifting as required.	Cable tension incorrect; cables damaged; derailleur damaged.	Adjust cable tension or replace gear-cable casing and inner cable. Replace the relevant derailleur.
Brakes do not offer the required stopping power.	With 'V' brakes, this can only be worn brake pads, or a contaminated rim surface or brake blocks. This may be true with cantilever brakes, too, but may also mean the straddle cable is at the wrong angle. With disc brakes, the problems may be as a result of air in the hydraulic system, or contaminated pads.	Replace contaminated pads and clean the brake surface with alcohol (take care not to get grease or oil on the brake pads, rim or disc rotor).
Chain jumping.	Worn chain; worn sprockets; new chain has not yet been ridden in enough to mesh with gear teeth.	Replace chain if it is not new, and/or replace rear cassette.
Suspension forks do not operate properly.	Need a service or oil change.	Service according to manual, or have forks serviced at a bike shop.
Brakes screech.	Pads need 'toe in' adjustment.	Adjust as required.
Rim rubs against brake pads.	Rim not true; brakes set too tight; quick-release hub skewer not tightened evenly.	True rim or loosen cable tension. Tighten quick-release hub skewer again. If all fails, disconnect brakes.

Emergency trail-side repairs

Knowing how the bicycle's parts fit together and having the right tools to do the job effectively will make the repair of your bike much easier.

It is, therefore, important — both for the maintenance of your bike and your own safety — that you know how to handle the most common difficulties and what can be done to resolve them.

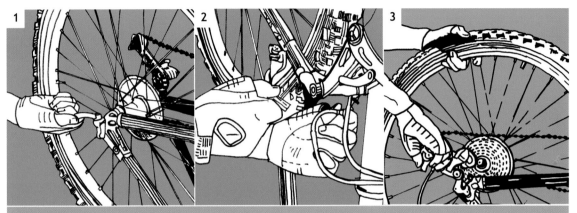

Removing the rear wheel

The back wheel appears to be a bewildering combination of brakes, gears, sprockets, derailleur and chain, so it is no surprise that many novice riders battle with this basic step. Shift the gears so the chain is on the middle chainring in the front and the smallest sprocket at the back.

1 Undo the quick-release lever on the rear hub. Flip the bike upside down.

2 Unhook the rear cantilever or 'V' brake cable.

3 Pull back the derailleur with one hand, while pulling the wheel out of the frame with the other. If the bike is equipped with disc brakes, take care not to pull the brake lever while the wheel is out of the frame.

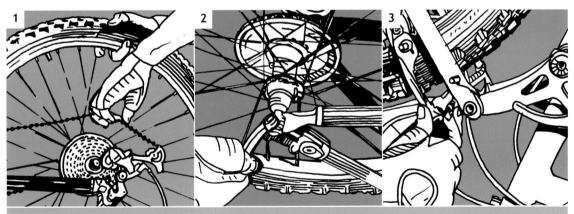

Putting back the rear wheel

1 Lift the chain coming from the top of the middle ring away from the frame. Position the wheel in the frame, with the smallest sprocket lying on top of the section of chain that leads to the bottom of the middle chainring.

2 Position the wheel in the frame drop-outs (where it is clamped or bolted onto the frame). Fasten the quick-release lever, but be sure to do so according to the instructions supplied by the manufacturer.

3 Reconnect the brakes. Flip the bike upright.

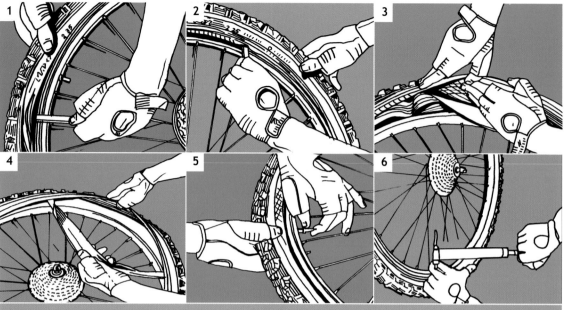

The dreaded puncture

A flat tyre may be caused by impact, a foreign object, or a simple cut. Remove the object if you find one, and use a flat rubber patch to temporarily repair a cut. If the tube has two small holes next to each other, it is probably an impact puncture where the rim bites into the tube. A large cut is seldom repairable, and the tube must be replaced. If you have no spare tube, and the existing one is beyond repair, you can 'limp' home by stuffing the tyre with vegetation, or tying a knot in the tube (where the hole is), and mounting it again.

1 Undo the brakes, loosen the quick-release, and take the wheel out. Use tyre levers to prise between the beading of the tyre and the rim.

2 Once the beading is over the rim, 'skin' the tyre off the rim on one side.

3 Feel inside the tyre and remove the objects that caused the puncture.

4 Remove the punctured tube. If you have a spare tube, insert this between the inside of the tyre and the rim, pulling the valve through the hole in the rim. If you have no spare, locate and fix the puncture (all repair kits have step-by-step instructions). Do not pinch the tube between the rim and tyre beading. Coax the beading off the tyre and back inside the rim. Use your hands to coax the last piece of beading into the tyre (stand on the stubborn section of tyre with your heel and lever the entire wheel to manoeuvre the tyre back).

5 Check the position of the valve. If it is crooked or pinched between rim and beading, push the valve up into the tyre (and pull it out again) to ensure that the tube is properly settled in.

6 Start pumping.

Pumping the tyres

A foot pump will make your task much easier. You can pump them to the right pressure, as indicated on the tyre sidewall, by looking at the gauge. Take note of what kind of valves you have — car tyre, Schraeder or Presta — and make sure that your pump has the right fitting or adaptor for these. If you are pumping by hand, here is the most efficient way to do it:

1. Remove the valve cap. If there is a screw on the valve, loosen it to allow the air to flow into the tube.
2. With the valve at the top, attach the pump.
3. Now hold the wheel with your free hand by placing your thumb on top of the tyre, and your index and middle fingers around the valve and the pump.
4. For support and leverage, rest the elbow of your arm holding the pump on your thigh. Start pumping.

A broken chain

The bicycle chain transmits the power you apply to propel the bicycle. Although a well-maintained chain should not break, a mis-shift can damage the chain and apply too much torque onto the drive train (largely because you are riding in the wrong gear).

1. You will need a chain-riveting tool.

Note: Shimano chains require a special pin to replace the pin pressed out in the procedure outlined above. In this case, you may press out the pin completely.

2. Press out the pins so that the damaged plates can be removed and you can match a link with outer plates to a link with inner plates.

3. Be careful not to press out the pin of the first undamaged link with outer plates. Leave enough of the pin so that one end remains stuck inside the plate.

4. To join the links, press the link back into position. To loosen a stiff link, grab the chain on both sides of the joined link and apply pressure laterally (and in the direction the chain was not designed to bend).

5. The chain is now shorter, which may limit the gear ratios you can now select.

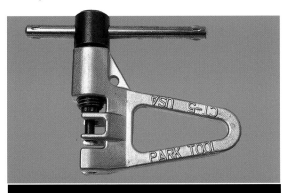

A SIMPLE, YET ESSENTIAL, CHAIN-RIVETING TOOL.

A buckled wheel

A slightly buckled wheel may be trued by adjusting the spoke tension, but if it has been warped ('pretzled'), you may need to have it rebuilt by a professional!

1. Unhook the brakes on the wheel, and check whether the wheel will pass through the frame. If it does, you can ride home like that. If not, you need to bend the rim back into shape using brute force.

2. Place the wheel on the ground and stand on the rim, using your body to bend the rim into shape. Although it will not be as true as it was when new, it should allow you to reach your destination if you ride carefully.

DARING EXPLOITS MAY BE FUN BUT CAN DAMAGE BICYCLE COMPONENTS.

Broken spokes

Unless you carry spare spokes for your wheels, simply remove the broken spokes and ride home slowly.

1. A spoke wrench will allow you to tighten the neighbouring spokes and keep the wheel fairly straight.

2. If the break occurred on the hub side, unscrew the spoke from the nipple and, if it broke on the rim side, thread the spoke out through the hole in the rim.

3. If the break is on the rear hub, you may not be able to remove the spoke easily. Wrap it around the next unbroken spoke to keep it out of harm's way.

A broken gear cable

A broken gear cable will usually mean that the internal derailleur spring will move it to the standard resting position. Limiting screws on the derailleurs can be used to set it in a fixed position to get you home.

1. If the front cable has broken, set the chain on the middle ring using the inside limiting screw.

2. If the rear cable has broken, use the limiting screw on the rear derailleur to set it onto one of the centre sprockets of the rear cassette.

3. To avoid injury, remove the broken cable.

Safe Riding!

true off-road riding is an exercise in self-exploration. There are no convenient road signs to tell you which way to go, or how far you still have to travel ... and, depending on where you live and ride, no trail markings or arrows to tell you what to do.

Road versus off-road cycling

Most mountain bikes never even get onto a dirt track, so it is up to you to decide whether or not you are going to exchange those slicks you bought for the original knobbly tyres.

Trail ethics

Like all knowledge and skill, you need to apply the advice and guidelines described in here responsibly. The image of risk and extremely high speeds is not what mountain biking is about; many off-road riders are parents with children, groups of friends out to enjoy the scenery, outdoor enthusiasts, or competitive cyclists participating in organized events.

To improve your skills, take part in organized off-road events because on the trail, you are in an uncontrolled environment and you will have to consider the needs of others too.

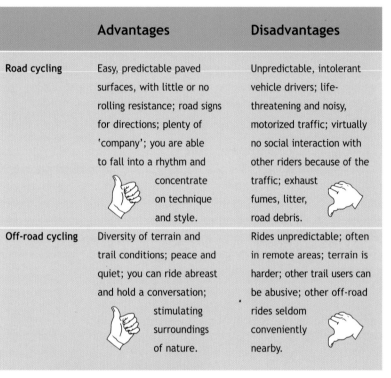

	Advantages	Disadvantages
Road cycling	Easy, predictable paved surfaces, with little or no rolling resistance; road signs for directions; plenty of 'company'; you are able to fall into a rhythm and concentrate on technique and style.	Unpredictable, intolerant vehicle drivers; life-threatening and noisy, motorized traffic; virtually no social interaction with other riders because of the traffic; exhaust fumes, litter, road debris.
Off-road cycling	Diversity of terrain and trail conditions; peace and quiet; you can ride abreast and hold a conversation; stimulating surroundings of nature.	Rides unpredictable; often in remote areas; terrain is harder; other trail users can be abusive; other off-road rides seldom conveniently nearby.

above FOR YOUR OWN SAFETY AND PEACE OF MIND, CYCLE IN GROUPS RATHER THAN ON YOUR OWN.
opposite CAREFULLY EVALUATE TRAIL CONDITIONS BEFORE YOU START — ESPECIALLY IF YOU ARE ALONE.

Horses are ponderous and slow and hikers walk at their own pace, so a fast and agile bicycle is certain to elicit a reaction from other trail users. Add to this the fact that there is not enough open space near cities, too few trails — and those that do exist are, as a result, rather overcrowded — and you have the breeding ground for intensified environmental impact and potential conflict. Listed on pages 78–79 are the trail ethics advocated by the International Mountain Bicycling Association (IMBA):

1. Ride on open trails only

Do not ride in an area closed to cyclists. If you are practising downhilling, make sure that there are no other users on the route and seek permission.

Other trail users

On an off-road trail, mountain bikers come face to face with the excitement and challenge posed by the rough, unpredictable terrain, but they may also encounter other trail users. As already mentioned on the previous page, mountain bikers often come into contact with both hikers and riders on horseback. These three categories of trail user generally have the same goal in mind: a relaxing outing in the peace and quiet of a beautiful natural environment.

In this context, it is clearly inconsiderate to ride recklessly in search of your particular kind of thrill or spill. Provided everyone acts considerately, and follows some very basic rules, there is no reason for conflict.

Sign language

Understanding the meaning of the special signs that are used, following signposts carefully, and keeping to demarkated routes provide a sound basis for happy trail sharing. There are at least two important types of off-road trail signs of which mountain bikers should be aware. These are:

Signs indicating yield

While out riding an off-road trail, you may encounter several multiple-use trail signs. The most common is a triangular sign with symbols in each corner representing a human (hiker), a horse and a bicycle. This is the sign to 'give way' or 'yield'. Whoever is at the apex of the triangle – usually the pedestrian – has right of way. The other two symbols on the sign will have arrows pointing away from them, indicating to whom they must give way. Sometimes, the triangular yield sign is used as part of a larger multiple-use sign, describing elements of trial courtesy.

Route markers

Mountain bikers participating in organized off-road events, and even along recreational trails, will see signs that show directions and warn of dangerous obstacles on the route.

 ### 2. Control your bicycle

Never ride fast along a busy trail. Ride slowly, keeping your speed, descents and braking well under control. Do not enter a blind corner at high speed unless you are competing on a closed and controlled course.

OFF-ROAD CYCLISTS OFTEN HAVE TO SHARE THEIR ENVIRONMENT WITH OTHER OUTDOOR ENTHUSIASTS, SO ALWAYS BE CONSIDERATE.

 ### 3. Always yield on the trail

A bicycle is silent and it is easy to 'spook' other trail users, especially if you approach from behind. Slow down to the pace of the equestrian or hiker ahead, and call for permission to pass. When granted, wait for a widening in the trail, passing at moderate speed with a thank you for their co-operation. Horses and dogs can be unpredictable, so if in doubt stop off at the side.

4. Never scare animals

Respect all wildlife, but be especially wary of wild animals in wilderness areas. See also Point 3.

5. Leave no trace

Keep your refuse with you and dispose of it once you get home. Also, be proactive: take a bag with you to collect rubbish you may find en route. If nature calls and there are no toilets, dig a hole or cover it with a rock. An energy-bar wrapper can disqualify you from a race as much as a puncture. Avoid riding trails after heavy rain as the terrain is usually soft and muddy and the impact of rolling tyres will create a rut that will get progressively deeper and wider. Besides, it's not good for the bike!

RESPECT THE GREAT OUTDOORS BY OBSERVING SIMPLE ETIQUETTE.

6. Plan ahead

Keep your eyes focused ahead of you and not on your front wheel. This way, you can anticipate what is happening on the trail. In the broader context of future planning, offer to help other trail users or land managers maintain the trail. Have vision!

The International Mountain Bicycling Association (IMBA)

The IMBA was initiated in 1988 as a coalition of Californian mountain-bike clubs to fight unwarranted trail closures by encouraging responsible off-road cycling and to advocate the rights of cyclists. Today, it is a multifaceted international association, with a mission to promote mountain biking that is environmentally sound and socially responsible. See page 93.

IMBA
International Mountain
Bicycling Association

International Alpine Distress Signal

The international signal to guide rescuers to your position are:

Whistle	six blasts
Torch	six flashes

Each is followed by a minute's pause and then a repetition. Any reply should come as either three blasts or flashes, repeated after a minute.

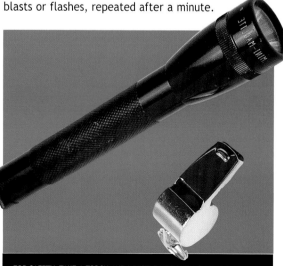

FOR SAFETY, TAKE A TORCH AND WHISTLE WITH YOU ON THE RIDE.

Survival kit

Long distance (80km/50 miles)

- Detailed map
- Cellular phone or satellite phone
- GPS or compass
- Mirror (or small pencil flares) to signal for help
- Bicycle light
- Matches
- Space blanket or two garbage bags (for shelter or emergency clothing)
- Waterproof windbreaker
- Penknife (or compact multi-tool)
- Whistle
- Extra food and water
- Pump
- Spare tube
- Puncture-repair kit
- Tyre levers
- Allen keys
- Chainbreaker
- Energy bar
- Money
- Personal identification with medical details
- First-aid kit

Short distance (25km/15 miles)

- Cellular phone or satellite phone
- Pump
- Spare tube
- Puncture-repair kit
- Tyre levers
- Allen keys
- Chainbreaker
- Energy bar
- Money
- Personal identification with medical details

THE OUTDOORS PROVIDES PLENTY OF OPPORTUNITY FOR ADVENTURE, BUT CAN ALSO BE UNPREDICTABLE. BE PREPARED AND USE COMMON SENSE.

A SURVIVAL KIT SHOULD NOT ONLY CONTAIN STANDARD ITEMS SUCH AS FOOD AND WATER, BUT ALSO EQUIPMENT FOR POTENTIAL EMERGENCIES.

SURVIVAL TABLE	Prevention
Animals The most common threat is 'man's best friend'. Most wild animals tend to avoid human activity.	■ Approach with caution. If a dog gives chase, dismount and put the bike between you and the animal. A mace spray is useful. When cycling in national parks, ride with an armed ranger, or go out in a group.
Criminals Criminals are predators who will go for easy prey. Many lie in ambush along popular trails.	■ Be vigilant, trust your intuition and avoid groups or pairs of loitering men. Never ride popular off-road trails alone. Never ride the same route, at the same time every day. Be sure to report all incidents.
Darkness Riding at night is dangerous if you do not have good lighting and reflectors. Reduced visibility off-road may cause disorientation.	■ Know how long it takes to do a ride, before you set off. In winter, because of reduced daylight hours, it makes sense to permanently attach front and rear lights to your bike. Wear reflective clothing. Ride more cautiously at night and at dawn. Avoid riding alone — especially in unsafe areas.
Head injuries Never ride without a helmet. You could easily have an accident 'just going to the shops'.	■ Learn how to fall properly, so that you hit the ground and roll, rather than land on your head. Cycle helmets cannot protect you against all injuries, but will minimize the damage. Treat your helmet as a safety belt.
Insects You may not realize you have been infected by a mosquito with malaria, or bitten by a spider or tick.	■ Depending on where you are riding, it may be a good idea to add an anti-histamine ointment. Spray yourself with insect repellent. If you notice a bite on your body, and you are not feeling well, visit a doctor as soon as possible.
Getting lost Plan your trip well! Bad weather and unknown territory are the main reasons for getting lost, but riders are also lost in familiar places.	■ Take an inventory of what you have, to gauge whether you have the capabilities of getting yourself out of the situation without help. Travel in one direction, or you may wander around in circles. Don't be distracted. Tell friends or family where you are going and when you expect to be back.
Mechanical failure A bike in bad shape *will* let you down.	■ Keep your bike in good shape. Never ride without tools and spares. Make sure you know how to address basic problems on your bike.
Motorized traffic You have to share roads with vehicles, which are the greatest threat to personal safety.	■ Ride *off* the road! Use designated bicycle lanes, and stay vigilant. Ride defensively, but never aggressively. Rather than give in to road rage, report reckless drivers. Keep well away from parked cars, to avoid getting 'doored'.
Radical riding Do not be pressured to tackle objects that will damage your bike or result in injury.	■ Ride the course before you compete in the race. Practise on obstacles you find hard to handle. Wear protective clothing. Ask an experienced rider to demonstrate how to ride it.
Remote trails Remote trails often entail long and difficult rides.	■ Tell somebody where you are going, and when you will return. Familiarize yourself with the area, and take sufficient supplies.
Vegetation Thorns, poisonous plants, fallen trees and protruding branches are the hazards of the outdoors.	■ Help maintain the trails you ride on. Line the inside of your tyres if there are thorns in your area. Carry a spare tube, puncture repair kit and pump. Anticipate the trail ahead, and do not blindly follow the rider in front of you.
Weather Weather can change unexpectedly, causing disorientation, hypothermia or heat exhaustion. Beware, too, of lightning.	■ Don't go out if the weather looks bad or may change. Speak to an authority who knows the area and its conditions well, and prepare accordingly: wear layers of warm clothing in the cold, and in the heat drink a fluid (with electrolytes) every 20 minutes. Ride in the morning to avoid the heat of the day.

Aches and pains

Cycle-related injuries can be categorized as traumatic (where your body hits the ground, trees or another rider) or non-traumatic (caused by overuse and abnormal stress on joint surfaces, muscles and ligaments). These can, of course, occur virtually anywhere — whether you are on a steep mountain slope, riding along the banks of a gentle river or on the busy roads of the inner city.

Cyclists who set up their bike correctly and cultivate good riding techniques should have few non-traumatic injuries compared to other sports.

KNOWLEDGE AND GOOD SENSE MAY PREVENT UNNECESSARY INJURY.

Problem	Solution
Chafing This is a very uncomfortable condition, usually in areas such as the groin, inner thighs, nipples, feet or neck.	■ Watch your personal hygiene. Keep your kit clean. Use an antibacterial wash on your body and clothes. ■ Before you ride, lubricate and protect potential problem areas with petroleum jelly or tea-tree oil. ■ Wear thinner, looser clothing in warm weather.
Eyes There are several threats to your eyes: sunlight, insects, vegetation, dust, stones and mud.	■ Buy two pairs of glasses: one to wear in sunlight, and another designed for low-light conditions. If you cannot wear glasses because of flying mud, turn your face to the side so your nose will 'shield' one eye. ■ Secure glasses to your head with a toggle string, so that they are easy to remove (and put back on) when they are misted up or are splashed with mud.
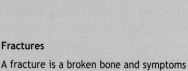 **Fractures** A fracture is a broken bone and symptoms include swelling, pain, immobility and, in a compound fracture, protrusion of the bone through the skin. The break most common to cyclists is the collarbone.	■ Care for the victim while waiting for professional medical attention. Fractures should always be set by a physician. ■ Watch out for shock and, in the case of a compound fracture, cover the wound with a clean cloth, bandaging snugly in place so that the pressure helps reduce the bleeding of an open wound. ■ Immobilize the injured area with a sling or a splint.

Problem	Solution

Headaches

Headaches may be caused by dehydration, or by too tight a helmet or headband. In hot, humid conditions, a biker can lose up to 2l/3pts per hour, but the body can only replace about 800ml/1½pts in an hour. Water takes about 20 minutes to reach any cell in your body. If you start adding sports drink concoctions to the water, it will take longer to enter into your blood.

- Before and after you ride, drink a litre of energy drink or water.
- While cycling — particularly if you are sweating — take an energy drink with electrolytes (to prevent cramps). Consult a professional, who may suggest a concoction of glucose, rehydration solution and water.
- After rides longer than two hours, drink plenty of fluids and keep an energy drink next to your bed.
- Make sure your headgear fits snugly, not tightly!

Head injuries

Drowsiness or loss of consciousness, even for short periods, are signs that some concussion may have occurred.

- Do not allow the victim to sit up or walk around.
- Keep the rider lying down and make sure that the rider's body is covered. This conserves body heat, and reduces the danger of shock.
- Do not give the injured rider any sedative, pain relievers or stimulants.
- When the victim must be moved, do it with the least movement of the body, and with the victim lying flat.

Knee injuries

Cycling is ideal exercise for the knees as it is non-weight bearing (and thus impact free), and does not extend the knee beyond its normal range of motion. Studies have, however, shown that 80 per cent of knee injuries are related to rider error. A bike is perfectly symmetrical, while humans are not, and any variations we may have (from a discrepancy in leg length to flat feet) is exposed during riding. On a two-hour ride, for instance, the knee bends about 10,000 times.

- Set your saddle to the correct height.
- Do not push big, heavy gears.
- Warm up properly.
- Keep your knees warm. When it is cold, the body sends the blood to its core — away from the joints.
- Wear long pants, legwarmers or calf-length pants when you cycle in cold weather.

Lower back pain

If you have been off the bike for a while, or are not used to off-road riding, you will probably suffer some lower back pain, which can spread down into the legs.

- Back muscles strengthen the more you ride.
- Your lower back is supported by your abdominal muscles, as well as back muscles. It is thus necessary to strengthen these in your training regimen.
- A quality dual-suspension bike will help alleviate lower back pain.

Problem	Solution

Neck pain

Neck muscles can become very sore when you hold your neck in an extended position for long periods — and this is precisely what happens when you cycle.

■ Check your riding position. A rigid upper body will manifest itself in hunched shoulders, adding strain to neck muscles. Relax your grip on the handlebars; drop your elbows and shoulders. Relax! Keep your upper body flexible.

■ Have your tight neck muscles massaged, or get into the habit of a gentle stretching regimen. An osteopath (if the pain is acute) or a physiotherapist can recommend neck exercises.

■ Should the pain persist, your neck may need to be realigned by a chiropractor.

Abrasions

Most abrasions are minor, damaging only the capillaries, and causing blood to be released into the surrounding tissues. Dirt, sand and other foreign substances may be ground into the injured area, contaminating the wound.

■ Holding the injured area upright helps stop the blood flow.

■ Abrasions need to be cleaned, and this may entail scrubbing them with a brush. A loose dressing should be applied to keep them clean.

■ Have a booster dose of tetanus toxoid.

Saddle sores

Saddle sores are painful boils between the legs that originate either from ingrown hairs or small cuts in the skin that occur as a result of friction and pressure between the skin and the saddle. These are infected by sweat and they fester, making it impossible to ride for a day or two after they appear. Other saddle-related issues are covered on pages 16 and 19.

■ Buy quality cycling shorts. Remove damp, sweaty shorts after a ride. Shower and change into clean, dry clothes immediately.

■ Make sure the shorts you are wearing have the appropriate chamois for your gender. See page 18.

■ If you have a saddle sore, let it come to a head and then lance it, applying an antiseptic afterwards. Wax the problem area to rid it of hairs that can exacerbate saddle sores.

Sunburn

Sunburn is the general term for inflammation and skin damage caused by prolonged exposure to ultraviolet light. It causes the skin to redden, flake and then peel off. There can be soreness, itching and even blistering.

■ Apply sunblock to your face and nose, arms, the backs of your hands, neck and ears, the tops and backs of your legs, and your shoulders. Cover scars with clothing or apply a full block-out, as scar tissue is sensitive to the sun.

■ Calamine lotion or ice will help soothe sunburn. Keep applying good skin-moisturizer to soothe and moisturize affected areas.

Problem	Solution

Stitches

This sudden, acute pain in your side is caused by an injury to the diaphragm as it is pulled up under the ribs.

■ Do not sit hunched over your handlebars. Straighten your back, open your chest area and give your diaphragm room to breathe.

■ Give your body time to warm up. Pace yourself and try not to ride beyond your own ability.

Sunstroke

The breakdown of the body's heat-regulating mechanism results in a dangerously high body temperature.

■ Heat stroke occurs when the body cannot control its temperature by sweating. Symptoms include hot, dry skin, headaches, thirst, nausea, dizziness and drowsiness. The temperature rises to above 40°C/104°F.

■ Heat exhaustion is caused by profuse sweating, and a loss of salts.

■ Remove the victim from the heat, undress the rider and wrap in a sheet soaked in cold water or place in a cold bath to get the core temperature down to below 38°C/100°F.

■ Symptoms include muscle cramps, headaches, vomiting, dizziness and pale, cold and clammy skin. There is a rapid pulse and the rider may collapse. Remove the victim from the heat, check the temperature and pulse and remove outer clothing. If the rider is conscious, give him or her salted water every 10 minutes to rehydrate.

Sprains

Ligament injuries occur when a joint is abruptly stretched beyond its usual range of movement. The fibres of the ligament tear, causing pain and then weakness in the joint itself. The ligament may even rip completely, leaving the joint vulnerable and unstable.

■ RICE — **R**est, **I**ce, **C**ompress and **E**levate — reduces swelling, internal bleeding and inflammation.

■ Anti-inflammatory cream may be required and you may need physiotherapy for ultrasound and movement therapy. Gently moving the injured limb will aid the recovery process and avoids muscle wasting or stiffness.

Wrists and hands

Aching wrists and hands are caused by the impact travelling up through the forks. It can also be caused by riding with rigid arms, gripping the bars too tightly and placing undue pressure on this region, or not altering your hand position. Brakes positioned incorrectly (so the wrists are bent when the forefingers are on the levers) may also be a source of wrist pain.

■ Fit suspension forks or a suspension stem.

■ Check your riding position and bike set-up: fit bar ends, so that you have more hand grip options; and make sure your brakes are in the 'attack position' (your wrists are in a straight line with the rest of your arm when your fingers are on the brake lever).

■ Buy comfortable gloves.

■ Take your hands off the bars occasionally and shake them to restore circulation. Hold onto the bars with heel of your hand, not with the sensitive area between the thumb and index finger.

The World's
Exotic Rides

from lush, green forests to dry, dusty plains, these rides are designed to whet your appetite and coax you off the road.

Finding the adventure

Finding out where to ride is part of the adventure.

Explore

Use your bicycle to run errands and explore the off-road options. Familiarize yourself with the landmarks and then, as you get fitter, extend your off-road rides further afield by connecting all your shorter routes.

Person to person

Establish contact with off-road riders familiar with the area. Cycling clubs and specialist cycle shops are a good starting point to root out devotees from transients!

Participate in events

Attend an off-road cycle event. They cater for different levels of riders, so don't be intimidated by the word 'race'. Riding with others is motivational too!

Cycle tours

Tackle an organized off-road cycle tour, and let a reputable tour operator worry about all the details.

The media

Cycling magazines — and the Internet (although few sites are updated regularly) — may provide event details.

Further information

Park authorities, tourism information centres and travel agents may also have some knowledge on mountain biking in their areas.

above EXPERIENCE THE REAL AFRICA AND SEE THE BIG FIVE UP CLOSE ON A RIDE THROUGH MASHATU GAME RESERVE IN BOTSWANA'S TULI BLOCK.

opposite LUSH VINEYARDS BACKED BY SANDSTONE MOUNTAINS — THE VIEW FROM BEHIND THE HANDLEBARS OFFERS AN ALTERNATIVE PERSPECTIVE.

Travelling with your bike

'I think I shall always stick to my bike,' said Christopher. *'The bicycle is the most civilized conveyance known to man. Other forms of transport grow daily more nightmarish. Only the bicycle remains pure in heart.'*

Iris Murdoch,
The Red and the Green

Sometimes, merely getting to and from your cycle destination can be an adventure. Although the bicycle is a mode of transport in itself, technology now offers several options for 'bridging transport' — whisking you and your bike to all corners of the globe.

By air

Terms, conditions and charges vary from airline to airline. Some large cycle organizations, which have sufficient clout, make arrangements with select airlines whereby their members can transport their bicycles free of charge. If you are not a member of such an organization, here are some 'flying lessons':

■ Get any agreement with the airline in writing — as well as a written receipt for any payment you make. This will help when you get to the check-in desk. However, decisions are often left up to the check-in clerk who may,

or may not, allow a little excess baggage free of charge.

■ Try to fly directly to your destination. Stopovers only increase the odds of losing your luggage. Cheap flights via three changeovers don't always work out the cheapest.

■ Sometimes, you may be able to take wheels on board the plane in wheel-bags. These may be stored safely behind the last row of seats.

■ Deflate the tyres and empty your water bottles. Wrap your frame in protective bubble wrap to prevent the paintwork from being scratched by friction and rough handling. Plaster your precious cargo with 'Fragile' stickers. Invest in a bicycle bag.

■ Fly Business Class if you need an increased luggage allowance, and join the airline's frequent-flyer program beforehand which may earn you more privileges.

■ For a good look at the best way to fly, what to fly and where to land, visit 'Travel with Bicycles — Airline Experiences' at the website www.GFOnline.org/BikeAccess/airlines.cfm

By car

Having your own car means you can go where you want, when you want. How you fasten your bike to your vehicle is up to you, and although many innovative cyclists design their own cycle racks, there are many bike

TO ENSURE THAT YOUR BIKE AND ITS COMPONENTS ARE NOT DAMAGED EN ROUTE, MAKE THE NECESSARY INVESTMENT IN RELIABLE BICYCLE TRANSPORT EQUIPMENT FOR YOUR VEHICLE.

transportation systems on the market. Consult your bike shop about which rack will be the best for your bicycles and vehicle.

By bus

There are few countries that actually offer this service on their buses. The bus is equipped with a rack at the back, where you can conveniently stash your cycle before paying your fare. In Third World countries, bicycles are stashed on the roof of the bus, or on top of (or underneath!) all the other passengers' baggage.

By ski lift

The world's leading ski resorts offer other activities when the snow melts, and mountain biking is often one of them. Why stress about riding uphill when you and your bike can catch a lift up to the top of each mountain — and just ride downhill all day?

By rail

Check with the relevant agent or service provider as to which trains and at what times you are permitted to take your bike on the train with you. This is particularly true of suburban lines — and especially during peak-hour commuter travel.

Bike hire

The quality and choice of cycle equipment for hire will vary with the demand. It is often more inconvenient to transport your own bike halfway across the world — not to mention the extra cost, and the risk. Hiring equipment is often more feasible. In countries with a culture of cycling — the UK and much of Europe — you can hire children's trailers, clothing and accessories. Make arrangements prior to your trip to ensure that you get what you want.

HARDENED CYCLING ENTHUSIASTS WHO MAY BE RELUCTANT TO TRANSPORT THEIR MOUNTAIN BIKE AND GEAR WITH THEM WHEN ON HOLIDAY, MAY CHOOSE TO HIRE A BIKE AT THEIR DESTINATION. WITH THE INCREASE IN POPULARITY OF MOUNTAIN BIKING, MANY MODERN ADVENTURE DESTINATIONS OFFER BICYCLE-HIRE FACILITIES.

Exotic rides

Cycling through wildest Africa or across the mountains of North America, every ride is an adventure.

Big Five biking

Where? Mashatu Game Reserve, Tuli Block, Botswana.
Why? Experience 'real Africa' from behind the handle-bars of a bicycle, covering vast distances through the bush, single-tracking along game paths.
When? March–September
Hospitality Luxury tented camp, all inclusive (daily charge for cycle rides if there are less than 10 riders). Entry-level mountain bikes available. Day rides – and a 40-kilometre/25-mile overnight ride – can be taken near the Motloutse River, where you can sleep in Tswana accommodation near the Motloutse Ruins.
Contact Joanne Lewis, tel: (011) 789-2677, fax: (011) 886-4382, e-mail: mashatures@malamala.com
Internet www.mashatu.com
Address PO Box 2575, Randburg, Johannesburg, South Africa 2125

Mountain madness

Where? Coastal and Rockies mountain ranges, British Columbia, West Coast, Canada.
Why? 2000km/1250 miles through multiple mountain ranges of back country in 27 days. Plenty of adventure activities and wildlife. Terrain varies from sea level to over 3000m/1850 miles, with a long stretch of a 10 per cent gradient and a few tame sections.
When? The snow has melted from the western mountain passes by late June, and by the time you get to the easterly end of the ride in July, those passes are also clear. Trips run regularly up to the end of August, and there are shorter sections on offer.
Hospitality Tented camps, all inclusive (except for a small daily bike rental). Gear is transported for you.
Contact John Sigurjonsson (Canadian Trails Adventure Tours), tel: (519) 352-0883, fax: (519) 352-2415, e-mail: canadiantrails@msn.com
Internet www.canadiantrails.com
Address Suite 153, 162-2025 Corydon Avenue, Winnipeg, Manitoba, Canada R3P 0N5

Volcano riding

Where? Iztaccihuatl and Citlaltéptl (Pico de Orizaba) volcanoes, Puebla and Veracruz, Mexico.
Why? Experience the altitude and incredible downhills of Mexico's highest volcanoes. Cruise Iztaccihuatl and traverse pine forest and arctic tundra areas above 4000m/13,000ft. Experience a high-altitude adventure of 3000m/9900ft downhills on the slopes of Pico de Orizaba in the bordering states of Puebla and Veracruz.
When? October–May
Contact Luis Reyes (Servimont), tel: (245) 15009, fax: (245) 15019, e-mail: 74173.2642@compuserve.com
Internet www.servimont.com.mx
Address Calz. Jesus Ortega #15 Tlachichuca, Pue 75050

Where? Mount St Helens National Volcanic Monument, Washington State, USA
Why? There are few biking trails open in this national monument. Towering above the floodplain is Mount St Helens, with glacier streams crossing the plains. At one point, a waterfall drops off the plain into a tree-filled

THE RUGGED MOUNTAINSCAPE OF AUSTRALIA'S BLUE MOUNTAIN RANGE IS AN OFF-ROAD CYCLING PARADISE.

valley. Another ride leads right into the blast zone.

When? May—August (northern hemisphere summer)

Hospitality There are several basic campgrounds.

Contact Mount St Helens National Volcanic Monument, tel: (360) 247-3900

Heli biking

Where? Mike Wiegele Helicopter Skiing, Blue River, British Columbia, Canada.

Why? Heli-biking is part of the summer activities at this ski resort in Blue River, some 600km/370 miles north of Vancouver. This spectacular 7770km^2/3000-square-mile terrain is a pure mountain-bike adventure.

When? July—September

Hospitality Log chalets on the shore of Eleanor Lake and a log-cabin lodge, with all the modern facilities.

Contact Mike Wiegele Helicopter Skiing, tel: (250) 673-8381, toll free (North America only) 1-800-661-9170, fax: (250) 673-8464, e-mail: mail@wiegele.com

Internet www.wiegele.com

Address PO Box 159, Blue River, BC — V0E 1J0

WITH WIDE EXPANSES OF ENDLESS SAND AND DESOLATE LANDSCAPES, THE DESERTS OF THE AMERICAS OFFER ENDLESS ADVENTURES.

WHEN TOURING EXOTIC DESTINATIONS, THE VERSATILE MOUNTAIN BIKE OFFERS A TACTILE ALTERNATIVE TO CONVENTIONAL MODES OF TRANSPORT.

Making contact

INTERNATIONAL BICYCLE FUND (IBF)

- 4887 Columbia Drive South, Seattle, WA 98108-1919, USA
- E-mail: intlbike@scn.org

Africa
Madagascar

ECOBOUND

- Tel: (+27-44) 871-4455
- Fax: (+27-44) 871-2274
- E-mail: ecobound@pixie.co.za
- Website: www.george/ecobound.co.za

Malawi

MOUNTAIN CLUB OF MALAWI

- Tel: (+265) 64-3436
- PO Box 240, Blantyre, Malawi

Namibia

NAMIBIAN CYCLE FEDERATION (NCF)

- Tel: (+264-61) 23-7728
- Fax: (+264-61) 23-8880
- E-mail: muirc@wce.com.na
- Website: www.namibian.com.na/cycling.html

South Africa

SOUTH AFRICAN MOUNTAIN BICYCLE ASSOCIATION (SAMBA)

- Tel: (+27) 082-651-8677
- Fax: (+27-41) 367-3021
- E-mail: lrossouw@global.co.za
- PO Box 28204, Sunridge Park 6008, South Africa

PEDAL POWER ASSOCIATION (PPA)

- Tel: (+27-21) 689-8420
- Fax: (+27-21) 689-8490
- E-mail: info@pedalpower.org.za
- Website: www.pedalpower.org.za
- PO Box 665, Rondebosch 7701

RIDE MAGAZINE

- Tel: (+27-11) 803-2040
- Fax: (+27-11) 803-2022
- E-mail: aftrac@global.co.za
- Website: www.ride.co.za

Zambia

LUSAKA LOWDOWN MAGAZINE

- Tel: (+260-1) 70-1397
- E-mail: lowdown@coppernet.zm
- Website: www.lowdown.co.zm

Zimbabwe

HARARE MOUNTAIN BIKE CLUB (HMBC)

- Tel: (+263-4) 74-4386
- E-mail: angiec@miekles.co.zw
- 151, The Chase, Mount Pleasant, Harare, Zimbabwe

Asia
Tibet/Nepal

HIMALAYAN ADVENTURES

- Tel/fax: (+27-11) 794-1348
- E-mail: jillpersson@netactive.co.za
- PO Box 454, Honeydew 2040, South Africa

Australasia
Australia

WESTERN AUSTRALIA MOUNTAIN BIKING ASSOCIATION

- Website: www.wamba.asn.au

PERTH MOUNTAIN BIKING CLUB

- Website: www.wamba.asn.au/pmbc/index.html

BICYCLE VICTORIA

- Tel: (+61-3) 9328-3000

BICYCLE NEW SOUTH WALES

- Tel: (+61-2) 9283-5200

FREEWHEEL MAGAZINE

- Tel: (+61-3) 9690-9065
- Fax: (+61-3) 9690-9068
- E-mail: freewheel@enternet.com.au
- 79 Canterbury Road, Middle Park, Victoria 3206

AUSTRALIAN TRAVEL INFORMATION EXCHANGE

- Website: www.atie.com.au

OUR AUSTRALIA

- Website: www.pecan.com.au/ouraustralia/index.html
- Website: www.alltrails.com.au
- Website: www.bicyclingaustralia.com
- Website: www.morning.com.au/go/wildtrails

New Zealand

DEPARTMENT OF SOCIAL AND CULTURAL COMMISSIONING, WELLINGTON CITY COUNCIL

- Tel: (+64-4) 801-3627
- PO Box 2199, Wellington, New Zealand

THE KENNETT BROTHERS

- Tel: (+64-4) 449-6376
- Website: www.mountainbike.co.nz
- Website: www.kennett.co.nz
- PO Box 11310, Wellington, New Zealand

Europe

France

FEDERATION FRANCAISE DE CYCLOTOURISME

- 8 Rue Jean-Marie Jego, 75013 Paris, France

FEDERATION FRANCAISE DE CYCLOTOURISME

- Tel: (+33-1) 3946-3919
- Fax: (+33-1) 4416-8899

LE TOUR VTT, SAINT ANTHEME

- Tel: (+33-1) 3913-3322

Italy

BICI DA MONTAGNA MAGAZINE

- Tel: (+39-0636) 30-9977
- Fax: (+39-6) 30-9950
- E-mail: bdm@cycling.it
- Website: www.cycling.it
- Via Della Maratona 66, 00194 Roma

Portugal

BIKE MAGAZINE

- Tel: (+351-1) 414-9900
- Fax: (+351-1) 414-0327
- E-mail: motorpress@mail.telepac.pt
- Rua Sacadura Cabral, 26, 30 1495 Dafundo

Switzerland

MOVE MAGAZINE

- Tel: (+41-31) 388-7272
- Fax: (+41-31) 388-7270
- E-mail: move@fischermedia.ch
- Website: www.move.ch

United Kingdom

England

BRITISH MOUNTAIN BIKING (BMB)

- Tel: (+44-161) 223-2244
- Fax: (+44-161) 231-0592
- Cycling Centre, 1 Stuart Street, Manchester, M11 4DQ

MOUNTAIN BIKE RIDER (MBR) MAGAZINE

- Tel: (+44-20) 8774-0811
- Fax: (+44-20) 8686-0947
- E-mail: mbr@ipcmedia.com

MOUNTAIN BIKE ROUTES UK

- Tel: (+44-1460) 74488
- E-mail: MBRUK@aol.com

North America

Canada

ONTARIO CYCLING ASSOCIATION

- Tel: (+91-416) 426-7242

ALBERTA BICYCLE ASSOCIATION

- Tel: (+91-780) 427-6352
- Fax: (+91-780) 427-6438
- Website: www.albertabicycle.ab.ca

CYCLING BC

- Tel: (+91-604) 737-3034
- Fax: (+91-604) 737-3141
- E-mail: office@cycling.bc.ca
- Website: www.cycling.bc.ca
- 332-1367 West Broadway, Vancouver, BC V6H 4A9

CANADIAN CYCLING ASSOCIATION

- Tel: (+91-613) 748-5629
- Fax: (+91-613) 748-5692

NORTH SHORE MOUNTAIN BICYCLING ASSOCIATION (NSMBA)

- Website: www.nsmba.bc.ca

United States of America

INTERNATIONAL MOUNTAIN BICYCLING ASSOCIATION (IMBA)

- Tel: (+91-303) 545-9011
- Fax: (+91-303) 545-9026
- E-mail: info@imba.com
- Website: www.imba.com

NATIONAL OFF-ROAD BICYCLING ASSOCIATION (NORBA)

- Website: www.usacycling.org

Glossary

26" wheels The standard size of mountain-bike wheels, 26 inches in diameter.

Adrenaline rush Euphoria experienced when, during periods of excitement, the brain secretes adrenaline into the system, causing an increase in the heart rate.

Aerobic A state of activity where there is an abundance of oxygen available for the body's metabolic process.

Anaerobic A state of activity where the body operates in a state where there is a shortage of oxygen. Usually a high-intensity exercise.

Air time The time spent in the air during a jump.

Alloy A metal comprising various other metals.

Bar-ends Extensions at the end of mountain-bike handlebars for a wide choice of hand positions and upper body comfort.

Bedded in Distributing your weight for maximum traction.

Berms A corner that has been built up to allow a perfect camber for high-speed cornering.

Big air Attaining considerable height during a jump.

Blowing up Indicating that a rider has come to the end of his/her endurance.

Bottom bracket Spindle and bearing assembly at the bottom of the frame to which the cranks are attached.

Burnout Overtraining, or when the cyclist continues to overload the body without planned rest.

Butted When the wall thickness of a tube varies from thick on the ends to thin in the middle. Provides weight saving, and offers a more lively feel.

Cadence Pedal revolutions per minute (rpm).

CamelBak™ Hands-free hydration system worn as a backpack.

Cantilevers Old-style rim brakes that cause resistance by pushing rubber pads against the rim. They are activated by a cable pulling the levers via a split cable running upwards from the wheel.

CE certification European safety certification for various consumer goods, including cycling helmets.

Chainrings The rings that are bolted onto the cranks which drive the chain.

Chamois The padded section in cycling shorts made from natural leather.

Choosing the right line The ability to discern the smoothest way through a rough section of trail.

Cleat Part under the shoe that clips into SPD-type pedal.

Cold-forged A part or component stamped into shape while cold, providing strength and better alignment of molecules.

Cross over Gear ratios that cause the chain line to sit diagonally from front to back.

Cruiser bikes A bike popularised by Schwinn for it's bow-frame construction. Usually used by recreational riders.

Dab Putting a foot down on the ground to control balance.

Derailleurs Move the chain from one sprocket to the next.

Disc brakes Brakes consisting of a metal disc bolted to the hub, and retarded by friction via a caliper unit mounted on the frame, which operates two or more pads pressed against the disc. Mechanically or hydraulically operated.

Downhill run A section of the downhill course as used in an official downhill competition.

Drawn, mitered and dressed tubes Mechanical actions or processes performed on tubing during the manufacturing.

Drive train The mechanical components that transmit the pedal force to the rear wheel.

Drop offs A term used to describe anything from a ledge to a steep slope down which you have to ride.

Elevation Height above sea level.

Energy transfer Transferring energy from your legs to the rear wheel to acheive forward motion.

Fat tyre Either a mountain bike or a mountain bike festival. The term is also used to differentiate between road cycling and mountain biking, or the terrain you ride on and the tyres you use. 'Fat tyres' usually indicate a mountain bike.

Field All the riders participating in an event.

Frame angles The angles at which the tubes actually meet relative to each other. This determines the way in which the bike will react handle and feel when ridden.

Frameset Assembled bike frame, excluding components.

Gear ratios Ratio achieved when dividing the size (number of teeth) of the front chainring with the size in the rear sprocket. The larger the number, the harder/faster the gear.

GoreTex™ Strong and warm space-age material with excellent water-repellent and insulation properties.

GPS Global Positioning System navigated by satellite. Usually portable, and invaluable if you are only using maps.

Grinding gears Turning the gears slowly under high pressure.

Groupset The gears, brakes, hubs, cranks, and other bike parts, excluding the frame rims, saddle and handlebars.

Hard tail A bike that has no suspension at the rear, but may have suspension on the front.

Heart rate Exertion measured, often by an electronic heart-rate monitor, by the number of heart beats per minute.

Holding your line To choose a line and commit to it. Also a warning shouted by riders who wish to pass, and don't want to be threatened by unpredictable moves.

Hybrid Neither a road bike nor a mountain bike. Used for commuting or by casual riders to experience both disciplines.

Lactic acid A waste or by-product of an anaerobic exercise.

Launch time The moment the bike leaves the ground at the start of a jump.

Linear, pull-type 'V' brakes A modern cantilever brake activated by a cable pulling the levers together from the side rather than from the top.

Mashing Pushing up and down on the pedals instead of pedalling in circles.

Pace To regulate the speed or rate of progress.

Pack Participants in a ride fragment into groups (or packs) according to their level of ability.

Panniers Strap-on bike bags used for touring, or commuting.

Pedal stroke The path or action of a pedal to complete a single revolution.

Platform pedals Standard flat pedals.

Power The combination of strength and speed.

Pre-ride briefing When the organizers of an event gather participants together and warn them of course conditions.

Pretzled wheel A wrecked wheel that resembles a pretzel.

Qualifying runs The test run to qualify for the final race (usually a downhill competition).

Radial configuration A spoke pattern where spokes radiate outwards from the hub, and not crossing each other at all. Usually used only on the front wheel.

Rear suspension A suspension system designed to allow the rear wheel to achieve suspension characteristics.

Recreational riders Casual riders with little interest in racing.

Riser bars Handlebars that rise higher than the stem for comfort (and fashion).

Road bike Drop bars, narrow tyres, big gears.

Seat tube The tube into which the seat post is mounted.

Snell 95 certification One of the best safety standards for helmets in the world. Certification is issued by the Snell Memorial Foundation; named after Johnny Snell who died from head injuries in an automobile accident in the 1960s.

SPD Shimano Pedalling Dynamics. A trademark of Shimano Corporation, but used generically to refer to clip-in shoes and pedals for mountain bikers.

Speed The 'speed' of a bike is determined by the number of sprockets in the rear casette. A 7-speed bike, for example, will have seven sprockets in the rear casette.

Spindle The central shaft onto which the cranks are bolted.

Spinning Pedalling more than 100rpm.

Splined A shaft or mechanical component with longitudinal cuts or serrations that match a complimentary component in order to prevent slippage and provide a firm connection.

Sprocket The metal discs on the rear hub over which the chain passes, driving the rear wheel.

Suspension fork The front fork of a bike, which has been specifically designed to work as a shock absorber.

Sweep riders A social ride will inevitably split into packs based on the ability of the riders, so sweep riders (who may be fit enough to lead) deliberately stay behind to 'sweep' up the stragglers and provide support.

Three-cross configuration A spoke pattern where each spoke crosses other spokes three times along its length.

Time trial An individual, non-assisted race against the clock.

Toe in Position of the brake pads relative to the rims. Setting the toes in and heels out will help prevent squealing.

Vert Abbreviation for 'vertical', describing steep downhills or drop-offs on a route.

Walking the course To closely inspect the cross-country or downhill course on foot to ascertain how to ride it, and to discuss which lines to take.

Weight distribution The percentage of body weight over the front wheel and the rear wheel. Usually 60 per cent over the rear wheel and 40 per cent over the front.

Wheel skewers The high-tensile metal bar that fits through the hollow axle, and allows you to fasten the wheel via a quick-release lever.

Wheelie The act of riding with your front wheel in the air.

Wash out When the front (or occasionally the rear) wheel slips out from under you as a result of a loss of traction.

Index

Photographic credits

Atra Corporation: p 8 (bottom); **Bob Allen:** cover, pp 8 (top left), 10, 23 (bottom), 39, 46 (bottom), 91 (top); **Sergio Ballivian:** pp 6, 38 (top); **Roger Brown:** pp 22, 25, 34 (top), 91 (bottom); **Cannondale:** pp 12, 13, 16 (bottom), 68, 86 (top); **Roger de la Harpe/Africa Imagery:** p 86 (bottom); **Ronny Kiaulehn:** p 19; **Jacques Marais:** pp 42, 61; **Tandem Association/Abraham Patrick and Faivre Hervé:** p 86 (top).